Past Masters
General Editor Keith Thomas

Bentham

John Dinwiddy is Professor of Modern History at Royal
Holloway and Bedford New College, University of
London. He was General Editor of *The Collected
Works of Jeremy Bentham*, 1977–83, and his publica-
tions include *From Luddism to the First Reform
Bill* (1986) and volumes vi and vii of Bentham's
Correspondence (1984 and 1988).

Past Masters

AQUINAS Anthony Kenny
ARISTOTLE Jonathan Barnes
ARNOLD Stefan Collini
AUGUSTINE Henry Chadwick
BACH Denis Arnold
FRANCIS BACON Anthony Quinton
BAYLE Elisabeth Labrousse
BENTHAM John Dinwiddy
BERGSON Leszek Kolakowski
BERKELEY J. O. Urmson
THE BUDDHA Michael Carrithers
BURKE C. B. Macpherson
CARLYLE A. L. Le Quesne
CERVANTES P. E. Russell
CHAUCER George Kane
CLAUSEWITZ Michael Howard
COBBETT Raymond Williams
COLERIDGE Richard Holmes
CONFUCIUS Raymond Dawson
DANTE George Holmes
DARWIN Jonathan Howard
DESCARTES Tom Sorell
DIDEROT Peter France
GEORGE ELIOT Rosemary Ashton
ENGELS Terrell Carver
FREUD Anthony Storr
GALILEO Stillman Drake
GIBBON J. W. Burrow
GOETHE T. J. Reed
HEGEL Peter Singer
HOBBES Richard Tuck
HOMER Jasper Griffin
HUME A. J. Ayer
JESUS Humphrey Carpenter
KANT Roger Scruton
KIERKEGAARD Patrick Gardiner
LAMARCK L. J. Jordanova
LEIBNIZ G. MacDonald Ross
LOCKE John Dunn
MACHIAVELLI Quentin Skinner
MALTHUS Donald Winch
MARX Peter Singer
MENDEL Vitezslav Orel
MILL William Thomas
MONTAIGNE Peter Burke

MONTESQUIEU Judith N. Shklar
THOMAS MORE Anthony Kenny
WILLIAM MORRIS Peter Stansky
MUHAMMAD Michael Cook
NEWMAN Owen Chadwick
PAINE Mark Philp
PASCAL Alban Krailsheimer
PETRARCH Nicholas Mann
PLATO R. M. Hare
PROUST Derwent May
RUSKIN George P. Landow
SHAKESPEARE Germaine Greer
ADAM SMITH D. D. Raphael
SPINOZA Roger Scruton
TOLSTOY Henry Gifford
VICO Peter Burke
VIRGIL Jasper Griffin
WITTGENSTEIN A. C. Grayling
WYCLIF Anthony Kenny

Forthcoming

BLAKE Marilyn Butler
JOSEPH BUTLER R. G. Frey
COPERNICUS Owen Gingerich
DISRAELI John Vincent
DURKHEIM Frank Parkin
ERASMUS James McConica
GODWIN Alan Ryan
HERZEN Aileen Kelly
JEFFERSON Jack P. Greene
JOHNSON Pat Rogers
LEONARDO E. H. Gombrich
LINNAEUS W. T. Stearn
NEWTON P. M. Rattansi
NIETZSCHE Ernst Behler
PAUL E. P. Sanders
ROUSSEAU Robert Wokler
RUSSELL John G. Slater
SCHILLER T. J. Reed
SOCRATES Bernard Williams
TOCQUEVILLE Larry Siedentop
MARY WOLLSTONECRAFT
  William St Clair

and others

John Dinwiddy

Bentham

Oxford   New York

OXFORD UNIVERSITY PRESS

Oxford University Press, Walton Street, Oxford OX2 6DP

Oxford New York Toronto
Delhi Bombay Calcutta Madras Karachi
Petaling Jaya Singapore Hong Kong Tokyo
Nairobi Dar es Salaam Cape Town
Melbourne Auckland

and associated companies in
Berlin Ibadan

Oxford is a trade mark of Oxford University Press

© John Dinwiddy 1989

First published 1989 as an Oxford University Press paperback
Reprinted 1990

British Library Cataloguing in Publication Data

Dinwiddy, J. R. (John Rowland), 1939–
Bentham.—(Past masters)
1. English philosophy, Bentham, Jeremy,
1748–1832
I. Title
192

ISBN 0-19-287622-8

Library of Congress Cataloging in Publication Data

Dinwiddy, J. R. (John Rowland), 1939–
Bentham / John Dinwiddy.
p.   cm.—(Past masters)
Bibliography: p. Includes Index.
1. Bentham, Jeremy, 1748–1832.   2. Utilitarianism.
I. Title. II. Series.
192 – dc19 B1574.B34D56 1989 88-30856
ISBN 0-19-287622-8

Printed in Great Britain by
The Guernsey Press Co. Ltd.
Guernsey, Channel Islands

Acknowledgements

The author wishes to thank Stephen Conway, Marco Guidi, Len Hume, and David Lieberman for allowing him to consult hitherto unpublished essays of theirs; to acknowledge a general debt to James Burns, Fred Rosen, William Twining, and other scholars associated with the new edition of Bentham's *Collected Works*; and above all to thank Herbert Hart, Oliver Franks, and Caroline Dinwiddy for their valuable comments on the original typescript of this book. The typescript itself was impeccably produced, from a tiresome manuscript, by Mrs E. M. Simpson.

Contents

Abbreviations

The following abbreviations are used in references to Bentham's published works:

B   *Works of Jeremy Bentham*, ed. John Bowring (11 vols., Edinburgh, 1843).

C   *Correspondence of Jeremy Bentham*, ed. T. L. S. Sprigge, I. R. Christie, A. T. Milne, J. R. Dinwiddy, S. R. Conway (London/Oxford, 1968–), in *Collected Works of Jeremy Bentham* (*CW*), ed. J. H. Burns, J. R. Dinwiddy, and F. Rosen (London/Oxford, 1968–).

CC i   *Constitutional Code*, vol. i, ed. F. Rosen and J. H. Burns (Oxford, 1983), in *CW*.

C/F   *A Comment on the Commentaries and A Fragment on Government*, ed. J. H. Burns and H. L. A. Hart (London, 1977), in *CW*.

Chr.   *Chrestomathia*, ed. M. J. Smith and W. H. Burston (Oxford, 1983), in *CW*.

D   *Deontology, together with A Table of the Springs of Action and Article on Utilitarianism*, ed. A. Goldworth (Oxford, 1983), in *CW*.

IPML   *An Introduction to the Principles of Morals and Legislation*, ed. J. H. Burns and H. L. A. Hart (London, 1970), in *CW*.

OLG   *Of Laws in General*, ed. H. L. A. Hart (London, 1970), in *CW*.

S   *Jeremy Bentham's Economic Writings*, ed. W. Stark (3 vols., London, 1952–4).

The following additional abbreviations are used in references to other primary sources:

BL   British Library, Additional MSS.

Dm.   Dumont MSS, Biblothèque Publique et Universitaire, Geneva.

ER   *Edinburgh Review*.

UC   Bentham MSS, University College London.

1 Biographical outline

Although Jeremy Bentham's life was not crowded with events and personal relationships, it was by no means as narrow and featureless as has sometimes been supposed; and his intellectual life—the story of his various writing projects and theoretical interests, and the ways in which they fluctuated and intertwined—is notably complex.

He was born in 1748 into a prosperous middle-class family. His father Jeremiah, a London attorney who inherited property and enlarged his fortune through dealing in real estate, was affectionate towards him, but demanding and insensitive. His mother was a kindly woman but was evidently overshadowed by her husband, and she died when Bentham was 10. He remembered his childhood—apart from visits to his maternal grandmother's house in Hampshire—as monotonous and gloomy; few children of his own age were ever asked to the house, and amusements in general were frowned upon. A frail, nervous, impressionable boy, a prey to nightmares and afraid of ghosts, he found his main sources of enjoyment in whatever books he could lay his hands on and in flowers and music. His intellectual talents revealed themselves at a very early age, and were encouraged by his proud father to develop as rapidly as possible. He started Latin at the age of 3, and at 7 was sent, with the sons of the gentry and aristocracy, to Westminster, where he earned some distinction by his precocity as well as by being the smallest boy in the school. He was unhappy there, however, and perhaps even more so at Queen's College, Oxford, which he entered at the age of 12. Much younger than most of his contemporaries and kept very short of money by his father, he lived an isolated and restricted life, and meanwhile gained little satisfaction from the desultory and pedestrian teaching offered by his tutors.

Thereafter he was destined for the law. His father hoped that he would rise to the top of the legal profession, and frequently urged upon him the value of 'pushing'. But although Bentham was called to the Bar in 1769 and was employed to give a few legal opinions, he never pleaded a case in court and soon gave up the idea of practising. He probably felt himself ill-suited to the competitive world of the courts, and he was deeply repelled by the nature of the law to which he would have had to apply himself: he saw the English legal system as an intractable and disordered accumulation of precedents and practices, shot through with technicalities and fictions and incomprehensible to everyone except professional lawyers.

In the formation of his own cast of mind, one important influence was his keen interest in science, especially chemistry and botany. He was attracted by the systematic and empirical approach of the scientist, contrasting this with the antiquarianism and chicanery which he associated with the common law. Another major influence was the writings of the *philosophes*, especially Claude-Adrien Helvétius and Cesare Beccaria. It is probable that he first encountered the phrase 'the greatest happiness of the greatest number' in the English translation (1767) of Beccaria's *Essay on Crimes and Punishments*, which helped to arouse his interest in penal theory. He was even more deeply impressed by Helvétius's *De l'esprit*, first published in 1758 and read by him ten years later. Here he found, somewhat untidily presented, several of the ideas that were to be fundamental to his own system; he recorded in later life that it was Helvétius who had inspired him with the belief that legislation was the most important of all earthly pursuits, and with the hope that he himself might prove to possess a special aptitude or 'genius' for work in this field. From the early 1770s the study of legislation was the central preoccupation of his life. He devoted himself not to practising law but to writing about it, and to writing not about law as it was but about law as it ought to be.

Early writings on legal theory

The period between the early 1770s and the mid-1780s was one of sustained and remarkable achievement in the development of his ideas. One of his earliest projects was the working out of what he called his 'Preparatory Principles'. He was convinced of the need to construct a new and systematic legal terminology as a preliminary to the comprehensive examination of the theory and practice of legislation which he intended to undertake, and his manuscripts contain a mass of definitions and analyses of the fundamental terms and concepts of jurisprudence. He also wrote in the mid-1770s a long critique of Sir William Blackstone's *Commentaries on the Laws of England*, the classic exposition of English law published in the previous decade. A portion of this critique, focusing on a short section of Blackstone's work which dealt with 'municipal' law, came out in 1776 as *A Fragment on Government*, the first book which Bentham published. The main part of the critique reached an advanced state but was abandoned sometime in the same year, perhaps because Bentham felt that it had been distracting him for too long from more constructive work; the *Comment on the Commentaries* was in fact to remain unpublished until the twentieth century.

Also written during the 1770s was a dissertation on punishments, in which he developed and schematized ideas which he had derived from Beccaria; and closely related to this was an analysis of offences, which was to form a significant part of *An Introduction to the Principles of Morals and Legislation*. The latter work, which also included an exposition and defence of his basic ethical position and a long analysis of the aspects of psychology relevant to legislative policy, was intended as an introduction to a detailed plan of a penal code. Although not quite completed it was put into print in 1780, but it was not actually published at this time. This was partly because the code itself was only partially written, and partly because Bentham found that what he had envisaged as the concluding sections of the *Introduction to the Principles*, dealing with the 'limits of the penal branch of jurisprudence', expanded uncontrollably.

He had not previously devoted a great deal of attention to civil law, and when he started to consider the distinction or relationship between civil and penal law he was led into a lengthy and complex analysis of how 'a law' should be defined and how a complete and coherent body of law should be structured. This exercise produced by 1782 a separate work almost as long as the *Introduction to the Principles*, to which he gave the title *Of Laws in General*. Like the *Comment on the Commentaries*, this work—now recognized as one of his most impressive achievements and as a remarkably original contribution to analytical jurisprudence—remained in manuscript until the twentieth century: Bentham regarded it as too abstract and abstruse to be worth publishing. He did have hopes, however, that on the Continent, where a philosophical approach to legislation was more favoured than in England, there might be an audience for the ideas he had been working out, and during the next few years (*c*.1782–6) he devoted himself to drafting in French—which he wrote fluently but somewhat eccentrically—a '*Projet d'un corps complet de droit*'. This material was never brought to a very finished state, but it was to be taken over by his Genevan editor and translator Étienne Dumont in the 1790s and was to form the basis for the *Traités de législation civile et pénale*, published in Paris in 1802.

Personal relationships

In a letter written in 1778 to a friend living in Russia, Bentham described himself as 'working hard, though in a manner underground, and without producing any apparent fruits' (C ii 100). This description could be applied in general to his work on legal theory down to the mid-1780s. What of other, less cerebral, aspects of his life during his twenties and thirties? One salient fact is that he had difficulty in making ends meet. His allowance of scarcely more than £100 a year was slender, and he had to supplement it by doing hack work as a translator. Moreover, his financial dependence on his father stifled what seems to have been his first significant love affair. In the mid-1770s he wished to marry Mary Dunkley, the orphaned daughter of an Essex surgeon, but his father opposed the match because of her lack of fortune, and Bentham eventually gave way.

For a somewhat longer period in the 1770s Bentham enjoyed

a close friendship with John Lind, a man ten years older than himself who had worked in Poland in the service of King Stanislaus and from 1773 was the King's unofficial representative in London. Bentham co-operated with him over several writing projects, and through him obtained some indirect contact with the world of high politics. At the beginning of the following decade, Bentham himself was transported to the fringes of that world, when he was unexpectedly taken up by Lord Shelburne. For years he had longed for some recognition of his talents, partly to allay his father's disappointment at his failure to pursue the conventional road to legal success, and partly to help him surmount his own chronic lack of self-confidence. His *Fragment on Government*, published anonymously, had attracted some attention and caused flattering speculation about possible distinguished authors, but sales had slumped when the true authorship was accidentally revealed. Acutely aware of being a nobody, he had wishfully taken refuge in drafting letters to great figures of the Continental Enlightenment such as Voltaire, d'Alembert, and Catherine the Great, in which he described the nature of his work and sought their interest and approval. He did receive encouraging replies from d'Alembert and Chastellux when he sent them copies of his *Fragment on Government*, but it was Shelburne, he recorded in later life, who first made him feel that he was 'something' (B x 115).

The Earl of Shelburne was an unusual Whig aristocrat. He had been Secretary of State for a time in the 1760s, was leader of a section of the Whig opposition, and was to be Prime Minister for a few months in 1782–3. At the same time he was an enigmatic and isolated man, who did not mix easily in society and was much more interested in new ideas than most members of his class. He had already patronized other intellectuals such as the Dissenting philosopher Joseph Priestley; and in 1781, impressed by the *Fragment on Government*, he sought out Bentham at his chambers in Lincoln's Inn and invited him to stay at Bowood, his country house in Wiltshire. For the next decade or so Bentham had a quite close relationship with Shelburne (created Marquis of Lansdowne in 1784), who seems to have regarded him with esteem and even affection. On two occasions, in 1781 and 1789, he spent several weeks at Bowood, and in London he was a frequent visitor to Lansdowne House.

It was through the Lansdowne circle that he was brought into contact with Étienne Dumont, thereby forming what was from the point of view of his own reputation the most important connection of his life. Also, it was during his spells at Bowood, which he later remembered as the happiest weeks he had ever spent, that he met the one woman, apart from Mary Dunkley, whom he seems to have deeply loved. In 1781 Caroline Fox, a niece of Lady Shelburne and Charles James Fox and sister of Lord Holland, was described by Bentham as a sprightly, good-natured girl of 13 with a 'womanly sort of bosom' and rather large teeth which saved her from being a beauty (C iii 95–6). She teased him a little, and they played music and chess together. The acquaintance was renewed in 1789, after which he wrote her several half-playful, half-romantic letters; but in 1792 his attentions seem to have become unwelcome and relations were broken off. They met again in 1805 when Bentham uncharacteristically accepted an invitation from her brother to dine at Holland House. She greeted him in a friendly way, and after several further meetings he made her an offer of marriage, which she gently but firmly refused. They never met subsequently, but when he was nearly 80 he wrote her a nostalgic letter, giving news of himself and saying that since they last saw each other not a single day had passed without her being in his thoughts.

One other, even more enduring and important, relationship of Bentham's should be mentioned at this point: that with his brother Samuel, who was nine years his junior and was to earn distinction as a naval architect and administrator. Bentham took a keen interest in his education and prospects, and encouraged and shared his enthusiasm for applied science and mechanical inventions. Moreover, he regarded him with deep affection and an almost maternal protectiveness, and the numerous letters he wrote to him are among the warmest and liveliest in his correspondence. In 1779, when Samuel was thinking of making a career in India, Bentham wrote: 'O my

Sam, my child, the only child I shall ever have, my only friend, my second half, could you bear to part with me?' (C ii 222). He approved, however, of the idea that in default of openings in England Samuel should seek a post in Russia, as this course would not separate them so irrevocably and might conceivably further his own hopes of securing the patronage of Catherine II. Samuel duly left for Russia and worked there throughout the 1780s. In 1785, when he was employed to manage and modernize the estates of Prince Potemkin in White Russia, Bentham decided to pay him a visit. He arrived after a six-month journey, having travelled by way of Paris, Genoa, Smyrna, Constantinople, and Bucharest; and he spent nearly two years at Krichev before returning overland through Poland, Germany, and Holland.

The middle years

The mid-1780s, and the visit to Russia, marked something of a caesura in Bentham's career. After some fifteen years devoted mainly to the theory of law and legislation, there was a shift in his attention to matters of a more practical kind, and to areas where the sphere of legislation intersected with, or embraced, what would now be called penology, public administration, social policy, and economics. One factor which encouraged this shift to a more practical orientation was his interest and involvement in Samuel's industrial concerns; it was on the basis of an idea supplied by his brother that he wrote, while at Krichev, his *Panopticon; or, The Inspection House*. In this work he described in detail how a prison (or workhouse, or factory) could be constructed on a circular plan, with a central observation point from which the jailer or superintendent could keep the whole establishment under continuous surveillance.

On his return to England, he was much excited by the opening phase of the French Revolution, and by the opportunities it provided for drafting reform proposals and attempting to secure their implementation in France. He composed and sent to Paris several essays and memoranda—on 'political tactics' (that is, the procedure of legislative assemblies), on judicial organization, and on his Panopticon prison scheme. The last two got as far as being put before the National Assembly, and it was partly as a result of these offerings—and partly through his friendship with the Girondin leader Jacques-Pierre Brissot, whom he had known in London in the 1780s—that he was made an honorary citizen of France in 1792. To his great disappointment, however, none of his proposals was actually adopted.

Still greater frustrations were in store for him in England. In 1791 he put before the Prime Minister, William Pitt (whom he had met at Bowood ten years before), a proposal for the construction of a Panopticon penitentiary in London, of which he himself would be the 'contractor' and manager. The Government's response, though not speedy, was initially favourable, and in 1794 an Act was passed giving powers for the purchase of a site for the penitentiary. But the implementation of the scheme was obstructed by the opposition first of the Spencer family and then of the Grosvenor family to the erection of a prison in the vicinity of their London estates; in 1803, after protracted attempts to induce the Treasury and the Home Office to put into effect the plan which Parliament had approved, Bentham finally had to admit defeat. He had devoted much of his time for twelve years, and a large part of the fortune he had inherited from his father in 1792, to an extremely disheartening enterprise, and he was left with an acute sense of the lack of accountability in the administrative system and of the facility with which private influence could override what he regarded as the public interest.

Another major project of Bentham's, which had connections with his Panopticon plan, related to the Poor Laws. In a series of articles in Arthur Young's *Annals of Agriculture* in 1797–8, he recommended the formation of a national joint stock company to which the management of all the 'burdensome poor' would be consigned. Workhouses would be constructed all over the country on the Panopticon model, and those in need of relief would have to enter these institutions, where they would be set to work to cover the costs of their own maintenance and to provide a profit for the company's shareholders. There is some evidence that his writings on poor relief had a subsequent influence, through Edwin Chadwick, on the New Poor Law of 1834, but they seem to have made little impact when they were first published. The third of his main concerns in this middle phase of his life was economic policy and public finance. Though he made two attempts, both of them left unfinished, to write a general treatise on the 'art' of political economy (that is, on the principles of economic policy), most of his economic writings consisted of proposals or critiques relating to specific issues, such as possible new sources of government revenue, devices for reducing the burden of the national debt, and means of controlling wartime inflation. Between the mid-1790s and the early 1800s he tried to interest ministers in several proposals of this kind, but here again he had little success.

How far should Bentham's middle age—the decade and a half preceding the abandonment of the Panopticon project in 1803—be regarded as an unproductive interlude in which he was diverted from the central tasks he had set himself as a jurist? It has been forcibly argued by L. J. Hume that these years were far from barren and that the attention he paid to prisons, pauper management, and political economy helped to give an important new dimension to his thinking. In addressing these subjects he needed to move from the level of theory to that of application, and in drawing up plans for concrete institutions such as the Panopticon and the National Charity Company he had to consider a new range of problems relating to administration and management; it was during these years that he worked out most of the ideas on bureaucracy—and developed also the mastery of detail—that were later to be features of the *Constitutional Code*, his principal exercise in substantive codification. On the negative side, however, there can be little doubt that some of his projects, especially the Panopticon, did absorb a great deal of time that might, from the point of view of his long-term vocation, have been more fruitfully used.

By the turn of the century he was still largely unknown. His *Defence of Usury*—an attack on statutory restrictions on interest rates, published in 1787—had had a minor success and been translated into French, but his *Introduction to the Principles of Morals and Legislation*, which had been published in 1789 after his return from Russia, had had a very small circulation. Most people who had heard of him would probably have associated him with his Panopticon scheme; and in 1800 he was warned by his step-brother, the politician Charles Abbot, that he was in danger of acquiring the reputation of a mere projector (C vi 342). During the next decade, however, his fame did begin to spread, more notably abroad than at home.

Dumont, in the *Traités de législation* which he produced on the basis of Bentham's unpublished writings in 1802, was remarkably effective in presenting his ideas in a coherent, comprehensible, and readable form, and the work was quickly recognized as one of major importance. In Paris, it was enthusiastically reviewed in the *Moniteur*, and the deputy who formally presented it to the *Corps législatif* in 1803 said that it might prove as valuable for legislators as Hippocrates' work had been for physicians. In Russia, it attracted attention in the reforming atmosphere of the early years of Alexander I's reign, and on the initiative of the famous administrative and legal reformer M. M. Speranskii a Russian translation was undertaken, which appeared between 1806 and 1811. Later, especially after its translation into Spanish in 1821–2, the work was to have a great impact in Spain and Latin America.

Another turning-point for Bentham came in the opening years of the nineteenth century. In 1803, at about the time when he finally gave up hope over the Panopticon, he opened a new chapter in his studies of jurisprudence by addressing himself to the linked topics of the law of evidence and judicial procedure. In the years 1803–6 he focused principally on the former, writing the bulk of the material which was later to be edited by John Stuart Mill and published in five volumes in 1827 as the *Rationale of Judicial Evidence*. On judicial procedure he was to write more extensively in the 1820s, but in 1806 a scheme launched by the then Prime Minister, Lord Grenville, for a reform of the administration of civil justice in Scotland, led Bentham to embark on a pamphlet which was published two years later under the title *Scotch Reform*; in this work his ideas on procedure—his criticisms of the existing 'technical' system and his proposals for a 'natural' one to replace it—were concisely presented.

One noticeable feature of his writings on evidence and procedure in the years 1803–8 was a new degree of asperity in his attitude towards the legal profession; he said in describing *Scotch Reform* to his brother that lawyers were 'treated throughout as the scum of the earth and the arch enemies of mankind' (C vii 425). He had long been aware of the importance of the vested interests of lawyers as an obstacle to law reform, but in these writings he was particularly caustic and persistent in attributing the abuses of the system to their 'sinister interest' and 'sharp-sighted artifice'. Earlier, the proceedings over the Panopticon had made him highly critical of the executive; in the 1800s he let fly at judges and professional lawyers; and by the end of that decade he was coming to see the *whole* of the country's ruling élite as a confederation of sinister interests. He wrote in a manuscript of 1808 that there was a 'conspiracy among the high and opulent to support one another against the low and indigent' (UC xc 90). In the following year he turned his attention to the legislature, and he quickly came to regard *Parliament* as the mainstay of the confederation or conspiracy he had begun to discern.

Transition to political radicalism

For most of the earlier part of his career he had not given much direct thought to forms of government or questions of political reform. He imagined that he would be able to enlist the support of existing governments for the legislative policies he favoured, and for a time he hoped that an enlightened despot such as Catherine the Great would take up his proposals and employ him as a codifier. But it should be noted that at the outset of the French Revolution he was briefly converted to democratic ideas. In 1788–9 he came to believe that the Bourbon regime was so riddled with abuses that it required drastic structural reform, and he wrote an essay arguing that the French should adopt a system of representation based on near-universal suffrage and the secret ballot. Within a year or so, he moved on to the view that similar arguments were applicable to England,

and he drafted a work in favour of parliamentary reform. After about 1792, however, he became deeply alarmed, like many others of his class, by the course of events in France, and especially by the threats to security of life and property that seemed to be developing there; and he reacted strongly against democracy. In these years of alarm he was planning a *defence* of rotten boroughs, and could write that however anxious he was to see a reform of the legal system he wanted 'no change in the Constitution or in the form of Parliament' (UC clxx 173).

There was a variety of reasons for his reversion to a belief in political reform in and after 1809. An immediate reason for his renewed interest in the matter was the fact that parliamentary reform, having been more or less submerged for fifteen years or more, reappeared at this time as a subject of public debate. Also, it was in 1809 that Bentham formed a close connection with James Mill, who was to be second in importance only to Dumont as a propagator of his ideas; Mill was already convinced of the need for political reform, and he may have encouraged Bentham to apply himself to this question. Thirdly, Bentham was distressed by the paltry outcome of the attempt to reform the Scottish judicial system, seeing this as attributable not only to the hostility of the legal profession but also to Parliament's indifference. At a deeper level, his own experiences and his mounting disgust at the shortcomings of both the judiciary and the executive had prepared his mind for the formulation of a *general* analysis of misrule; and indeed in his unpublished writings of the French Revolution period he had gone some way towards framing an analysis of this kind, and a set of political remedies based on the principle that 'the stricter the dependence of the governors on the governed, the better will the government be' (UC cxxvi 12). Although in the early nineteenth century he did not apparently make any direct use of the writings of 1789–90, many of the arguments he expressed corresponded closely to those he had drafted earlier. Still, it was in 1809 and the succeeding years that the definitive change of stance took place. He had been a consistent radical in regard to the law for three or four decades: at this point his radicalism became explicitly and pervasively political.

This radicalism did not mean that he became obsessed with the reform of the system of representation. He did write at some length on this subject in 1809–10, and in 1817 he published a long pamphlet entitled *Plan of Parliamentary Reform, in the form of a Catechism*, which he followed up in 1819 with a complete draft of a *Radical Reform Bill*. He had come to believe that what he called 'democratic ascendency' was the most basic means of securing good government. Yet he recognized that misrule in England had many sources and supports apart from the inadequacy of the electoral system, and that many of these were in fact major obstacles to the widespread public recognition of the need for political reform. In the second decade of the nineteenth century he addressed himself to a wide range of topics, and his interests seem at first sight to have been diffuse, but one theme or strategy which linked many of them together was a general concern to explore and combat the methods whereby the 'ruling few' maintained their domination over the 'subject many'.

These methods included not only the kind of political corruption which the opposition Whigs had long criticized: the 'influence of the Crown', or the executive's use of patronage to influence the behaviour of MPs and voters. They also included the means by which the ruling few acted on public opinion in such a way as to make people accept and even respect the existing system of government and distribution of power. In his writings on religion, for instance, some of which were published under the title *Church of Englandism* in 1818, Bentham attacked the established church as a close ally of the political élite, criticizing the tendency of its teaching to instil intellectual submissiveness. In his work on 'fallacies'—most of which was written in this decade, although the *Book of Fallacies* was not published until 1824—he set out to expose the various types of specious and tendentious argument used by opponents of reform. In his more technical studies of language and logic—to which he devoted much of his time in 1814, though they were not carried through to the stage of publication—he was settling his own ideas about the abuse of language and about the modes of analysis and discourse best calculated to promote clarity of perception and communication.

Codification of the law

While writing about parliamentary reform and the various forms of 'corruption' and 'delusion', Bentham was giving fresh attention to codification, which had always been his chief underlying interest but from which he had been somewhat distracted since the 1780s by matters of less general scope. He had long hoped that he would receive a definite invitation or commission to produce a code of laws for a particular state, and he believed that such a request would provide the stimulus he needed to undertake the sustained and demanding labour which the task required. By the second decade of the nineteenth century, when he was in his sixties, he seems to have become convinced that if such an opportunity was to materialize before it was too late, he must actively seek to create it. In 1811 he was writing at great length to President Madison offering to draw up a comprehensive code for the United States, and in 1814 he was making a similar offer to Alexander I of Russia. In 1816 he at length received a reply from Madison, which was in essence a polite refusal but which expressed the hope that although Bentham's services could not be accepted in the mode suggested the fruits of his labours might in some other way be useful to America. Bentham interpreted this as a recommendation to approach the individual states of the Union, and he proceeded to write another proposal addressed to 'the citizens of the several American United States', which was printed with a number of supporting documents (including the correspondence with Madison) and circulated to each of the state governors. A further work, similar though more widely targeted, was printed in 1822 under the title *Codification Proposal, addressed by Jeremy Bentham to all Nations professing Liberal Opinions.*

It was in 1822 that Bentham began working in earnest on his *Constitutional Code*, and the impulse which set him going came from the Iberian peninsula. In the 'triennium', the period of liberal government which began with the Spanish and Portuguese revolutions of 1820, his ideas attracted considerable attention. Toribio Nuñez, librarian at the University of Salamanca, produced two volumes which attempted (very successfully in Bentham's opinion) to present the essence of his ideas, and Ramón Salas, professor of law at the same university, completed the first Spanish translation of the *Traités de législation*. Nuñez and Salas both became members of the Cortes, and in 1821 the president of that body sent Bentham the draft of a new penal code and asked for his comments on it. The Portuguese Cortes went one better than that. Bentham having sent over a collection of his works and an offer to draw up codes of law for the new regime, the Cortes not only ordered that his works should be translated into Portuguese but also accepted his offer to submit a set of codes, thereby providing the invitation that he had long been waiting for.

The Portuguese regime, like the Spanish, succumbed to counter-revolution in 1823, but Bentham's hopes of gaining adoption for his code were kept alive by developments in Greece, where the war of independence was proceeding against Turkey. His interest in Greece was particularly stimulated by two disciples of his, John Bowring and Edward Blaquière, who had become keen supporters of the cause of Greek independence, and in 1823–4 he was actually sending draft instalments of the *Constitutional Code* to Greece for the benefit of the provisional government. When it became fairly clear that the chances of his code being introduced there were remote, he transferred his hopes to the new states of Latin America, in which he already had some important contacts and followers. He had known Bernardino Rivadavia (President of Argentina 1826–7) since 1818, and had corresponded spasmodically since 1820 with Simón Bolívar (President of Colombia 1821–30); Rivadavia was an avowed admirer of his ideas, as was Francisco de Paula Santander, who was Vice-president of Colombia from 1821 to 1828 and subsequently President of New Granada. In a long letter to Bolívar in August 1825, Bentham said that of all states in the world Colombia seemed to him the one in which the enlightenment of the 'ruling

15

few' was most likely to make his *Constitutional Code* accept-able. Three years later, however, Bolívar, having become con-vinced that post-liberation conditions required strong govern-ment and the suppression of liberal ideas, decreed that Bentham's works should no longer be used for teaching in Colombian universities.

The *Constitutional Code* was merely one of several codes which Bentham envisaged as forming his 'Pannomion' or com-plete body of laws, but it was the only branch that he carried to a stage of near-completion: the first volume was printed in 1827 and published in 1830, and the material for the other two projected volumes reached a sufficiently advanced state to be put together in coherent form after his death. However, he did not concentrate exclusively on this code during the 1820s. He drafted substantial portions of the procedure code and the penal code, and although he made less progress in the actual drafting of the civil code he wrote a considerable amount of material relating to it in 1828–30. In addition, encouraged by the active interest in law reform that was being shown in England by public men such as Sir Robert Peel and Henry Brougham, he bombarded them with letters of advice and exhortation, and produced a series of pamphlets in which he criticized the cur-rent attempts at reform and advocated more drastic and systematic measures.

Old age and public recognition

The last twenty years or so of Bentham's long career were remarkably productive. They were also, it would appear, the happiest of his life (with the possible exception of his Bowood period). Physically, in contrast to his frailty as a child, he enjoyed a vigorous old age, suffering from minor ailments but playing fives and shuttlecock and jogging for the sake of his health. (John Neal, a young American who was staying with him in 1826, recorded in his diary one day in August that Bentham, aged 78, had just 'trotted' all the way from Fleet Street to Queen's Square Place on the south side of St James's Park.) Financially he was well off, Parliament having voted him £23,000 in 1813 to compensate him for the non-implementation of his Panopticon scheme. In the years 1814–18 he was able to rent a magnificent house in the west country, Forde Abbey, where he spent his summers and autumns, usually accompanied by James Mill and his family. He did not relax his habits of work while he was there, but he entertained a number of guests including the MPs Francis Horner, Sir Samuel Romilly, and Joseph Hume, the economists David Ricardo and Jean-Baptiste Say, and the Westminster radical Francis Place.

At Queen's Square Place, Westminster, the house he had inherited from his father, he cultivated a reputation for being reclusive and inaccessible, which may have helped to protect him against unwanted intrusions. But in fact a steady stream of visitors was admitted to his 'hermitage': mainly people from whom he wanted information or whom he hoped to influence, and members of the devoted group of followers which he had attracted by the 1820s. By then, although none of his grand legislative schemes had been realized, he had acquired considerable fame at home as well as abroad. The *Westminster Review*, which he helped to launch with his own money in 1823, propagated Benthamite or utilitarian principles in rivalry with the established Whig and Tory quarterlies; several other journals or newspapers were committed, or at least friendly, to the same principles; and the Whig Henry Brougham—in spite of Bentham's public hostility to the Whigs during his radical phase—could write in 1830 that his exposure of the defects of the English legal system was 'the greatest service ever rendered to the country . . . by any of her political philosophers' (ER li 481–2). Meanwhile, tributes arrived in profusion from overseas. The American Edward Livingston, himself one of the outstanding codifiers of the nineteenth century, described Bentham as 'the man who has thrown more light on the science of legislation, than any other in ancient or modern times'; and José del Valle of Guatemala, in a letter of 1825, gave him the sonorous title of '*legislador del mundo*' (UC xii 346).

Bentham's private style in these years of public recognition was light-hearted and whimsical. He had a favourite walking stick named Dapple (after Sancho Panza's mule), an ancient cat—he was always fond of animals—called the Reverend Dr John Langborn, and a jokey vocabulary for use in his own circle which included expressions like 'antejentacular circumgyration', meaning a walk before breakfast. Some people—as in earlier years, when Brissot had written of his 'angelic' character and Aaron Burr of his 'inexhaustible goodness'— found him very engaging and were deeply impressed by his benevolence. Neal, for example, described him as 'a man whom it were impossible to know without loving and revering him'. There were others who found him less attractive, and as an old man he certainly had serious failings. He was vain and egocentric, and surrounded himself with uncritical admirers much younger than himself, of whom the most favoured from 1820 onwards was Bowring. With friends who were closer to his own age and stature he tended to quarrel, as he did with James Mill and Dumont, and he could be ungenerous and ungrateful. When Dumont applied to him for help in 1820–1 over a projected penal code for Geneva he was unresponsive, apparently because he regarded the Genevan republic as too small and unimportant to claim his attention when he was busy with other schemes of greater potential scope.

In regard to his vanity, perhaps the most striking manifestation of his passion for self-advertisement was—and is—the 'Auto-Icon'. Interested in the technique used by the Maoris of New Zealand for dehydrating and preserving the heads of their dead, Bentham thought that the same practice could usefully be adopted in Europe, and that the preserved heads or auto-icons of great benefactors of mankind could be a direct inspiration to later generations. He directed in his will that his physical remains should be preserved and displayed; and his skeleton, filled out with straw and topped with a wax head (because the attempt to preserve the original one was not very successful), sits in his original clothes in a glass box in University College London.

His ambition to be remembered as the most 'effectively benevolent' person who had ever lived was a noble one. But his eccentricities and faults, especially in old age, made him easy to caricature and disparage, and contemporaries of his who were hostile to utilitarianism sometimes used his personal weaknesses to help discredit his ideas. These attacks, though they probably had some impact at the time, can be discounted in a longer perspective, but a more serious and influential attempt to link Bentham's limitations as a philosopher to his limitations as a person—or at least to the limitations of his personal experience—was made by someone who was largely in sympathy with him, John Stuart Mill. In one of two extremely interesting essays which he wrote about Bentham after his death, Mill applauded many of his ideas and achievements, but portrayed him as childlike, cloistered, equable, and emotionally shallow—as someone who had never known adversity or dejection, and whose knowledge of human affairs and human nature was very confined. There was some truth in the portrait as applied to Bentham in the years when Mill, born in 1806, had known him, and there was also much cogency in Mill's partly critical comments on his thought (of which more will be said later). But Mill underestimated the range of emotions which Bentham had experienced, and he was certainly exaggerating when he said that Bentham had been 'secluded in a peculiar degree, by circumstances and character, from the business and intercourse of the world'. Not many philosophers—though Mill himself was one of the exceptions—have had as much contact with the world of affairs as Bentham did.

2 The greatest happiness principle

In this chapter and the next we shall examine, first, the moral theory on which the whole of the rest of Bentham's thought was founded, and then some of the methodological approaches which he used in applying his basic principle and in criticizing existing modes of discourse and institutions. We shall then proceed, in Chapters 3–5, to consider his views on law, politics, and social and economic policy.

His best-known work in English, *An Introduction to the Principles of Morals and Legislation*, begins with some arresting but somewhat misleading sentences:

> Nature has placed mankind under the governance of two sovereign masters, *pain* and *pleasure*. It is for them to point out what we ought to do, as well as to determine what we shall do. On the one hand the standard of right and wrong, on the other the chain of causes and effects, are fastened to their throne.

It is clear that Bentham did not attach great analytic weight to these remarks, for he went on to say at the end of his opening paragraph: 'But enough of metaphor and declamation: it is not by such means that moral science is to be improved.' However, these sentences have encouraged many people to think that Bentham was guilty of confusing what is with what ought to be, or of deriving what ought to be from what is.

In fact, Bentham was well aware of the need to distinguish between factual or descriptive statements on the one hand and normative or evaluative statements on the other. He gave credit to Hume for having emphasized the importance of the distinction, and he actually wrote in one of his early manuscripts: 'It is my care throughout to keep distinct by every attention possible those two ideas so apt to be confounded, the idea of what *is*, from the idea of what *ought to be*' (B viii 128 n; UC lxix 89). His own philosophy was partly based on a factual statement, and partly on a normative one. The factual statement or assumption was that what people seek is their own pleasure or happiness; the normative statement or principle—usually known as the principle of utility—can be summarized (pending further explanation later in this chapter) as the principle that every action should be judged right or wrong according to how far it tends to promote or damage the happiness of the community, or the happiness of those people whom the action affects.

Bentham did not claim that the second statement could be *logically* deduced from the first; he recognized, and explicitly stated, that the principle of utility was a postulate of which the truth could not be *proved*. However, he did set out to devise a theory of morals which *accorded with* the observable facts of human nature (as he saw them), and which did not need any recourse to concepts that were religious or mysterious. True knowledge, he believed, was derived from 'feelings and experience', and he wished to construct a theory of morals and legislation on this 'immovable base' (B i 304). He wrote in the *Rationale of Judicial Evidence*:

> In morals, as in legislation, the *principle of utility* is that which holds up to view as the only sources and tests of right and wrong, human suffering and enjoyment—pain and pleasure. It is by experience, and that alone, that the tendency of human conduct, in all its modifications, to give birth to pain and pleasure, is brought to view: it is by reference to experience, and to that standard alone, that the tendency of any such modifications to produce more pleasure than pain, and consequently to be *right*—or more pain than pleasure, and consequently to be *wrong*—is made known and demonstrated. (B vi 238)

Before examining in more detail the ways in which his theory of psychology was linked to his theory of ethics, let us briefly consider each of these in turn, beginning with his theory of human nature and motivation. His basic assumption about behaviour was that all actions—all, at least, that were the

21

Bentham

outcome of human will—were motivated by the desire to obtain some pleasure or to avoid some pain. Pleasures and pains were broadly interpreted; he once wrote, following the French philosopher Maupertuis: 'I call pleasure every sensation that a man had rather feel at that instant than feel *none*. I call pain every sensation that a man had rather feel none than feel' (UC xcvi 128). The great range of pleasures and pains by which people could be motivated—in other words, the great range of *motives*—was analysed and classified in two of Bentham's works, *An Introduction to the Principles of Morals and Legislation* and *A Table of the Springs of Action* (1815). In the former he divided motives into three general categories, social, dissocial, and self-regarding. The social category was subdivided into the purely social and the semi-social; and the one motive that was described as *purely* social was goodwill. This was the motive that corresponded to the pleasures (and pains) of sympathy: the pleasures (or pains) that an individual derived from contemplating the happiness (or unhappiness) of others, without himself being influenced by any ulterior view with respect to his own self-regarding interest. The motives described as semi-social were the love of reputation, the desire of amity, and the motive of religion. They each had a social tendency, a tendency to promote the happiness of others, but they were all 'self-regarding at the same time' (the self-regarding aspect of the religious motive being the desire to earn salvation or to avoid divine punishment). The dissocial motive included in the classification was termed 'the motive of displeasure', and was associated with the pleasures and pains of antipathy and resentment. Lastly, the self-regarding motives were listed as physical desire, pecuniary interest, love of power, and self-preservation (the last embracing the fear of pain, the love of ease, and the love of life).

According to his analysis, even the social motive of goodwill was identified with a desire *on the part of the agent* to obtain pleasure or avoid pain for himself. As he put it in a memorandum written forty years later: 'If it be through the happiness of another, or others, in whatsoever number, that a man pursues his own happiness, still the direct and immediate, and nearest object is not the less his own happiness' (B x 532). In this sense Bentham's psychology was egoistic, but it by no means ruled out the possibility of benevolent conduct. An idiosyncrasy of his vocabulary which may have helped to obscure this fact is the use he made of the word 'interest'. He maintained that for *every* motive there was a corresponding interest; he could thus write in a manuscript of 1816: 'Of every human being the conduct is on every occasion at any moment determined by the conception which at that moment he has of his individual interest' (UC xviii 173). But interest was not to be equated with 'self-interest' in the usual sense (indeed, this was a term that Bentham avoided). Even if a person performed an action from the 'purely social motive of sympathy or benevolence', he expected to obtain pleasure or gratification from doing so, and he had as much of an interest in performing the action concerned as he did when he performed an action from self-regarding motives. The interest corresponding to the motive of goodwill was described by Bentham as a 'social' rather than a 'self-regarding' one; but statements of his to the effect that every man's conduct was determined by 'interest' have helped to create the impression that he subscribed to a cruder version of egoistic hedonism than in fact he did.

One other point that is worth making about the role of sympathy and benevolence in Bentham's system is that in his later writings—including his *Deontology*, the unfinished work on 'private ethics' on which he worked spasmodically from 1814 onwards—he gave sympathy a somewhat more prominent place in his theory of motivation than he had earlier. In the *Introduction to the Principles* he devoted a chapter to what he called 'the four sanctions or sources of pain and pleasure'. A sanction—a term which he borrowed from the vocabulary of law and applied more broadly—was defined as a source of pains and pleasures, and thus of motives: or, in a later work, as a source of 'obligation and inducement' (B iii 290). The first of these was the physical sanction: the source of those impulsions and constraints which arose from man's nature and natural circumstances. The second was the political, including the legal, sanction: the source of those influences on behaviour which took the form of punishments and rewards ordained or supplied by political authority. The third was the moral or popular sanction, which denoted the influences on behaviour that were exerted by collective opinion, or by the approval and disapproval of those with whom a person happened to be in contact. And the fourth was the religious sanction, from which emanated the motives constituted by the hope of divine reward and the fear of divine punishment. (Bentham did not consider that much reliance could be placed on this fourth sanction.)

In the analysis in the *Introduction to the Principles*, the pleasures and pains of sympathy and the motive of benevolence were treated as a branch of the physical sanction: that is, as arising from the natural constitution of man. In 1814, however, he added to the original list a fifth sanction, the sanction of sympathy. He had come to think that sympathetic feelings, aroused by the consideration of a pleasure or pain being experienced or about to be experienced by another person, were so different from pleasures or pains of an entirely self-regarding kind, that the source of such feelings and of the motives associated with them ought to be classified separately; and he added that 'were it not for the operation of this sanction, no small portion of the good, physical and moral, which has place in human affairs, would be an effect without a cause' (B iii 292).

At this juncture, however, the crucial point needs to be made that in Bentham's view the force of the sympathetic sanction and of benevolent motives was not generally very strong. He wrote in the *Introduction to the Principles* (155) that 'the motives, whereof the influence is at once most powerful, most constant, and most extensive, are the motives of physical desire, the love of wealth, the love of ease, the love of life, and the fear of pain: all of them self-regarding motives'. More than forty years later he wrote similarly, in the prefatory section of the *Constitutional Code*, that 'in the general tenor of life, in every human breast, self-regarding interest is predominant over all other interests put together' (B ix 5); and many other statements to the same effect are to be found scattered through his writings. He recognized that in exceptional cases the social affections could have a major influence on conduct; he said in a work published in 1830: 'I admit the existence of *philanthropy* . . . I have not far to look for it' (!) (B iv 431). But he thought that as a general rule the 'principle of self-preference', as he called it, held good, and should be treated for the purposes of legislation and social management as a basic fact of human nature.

His theory of ethics

Let us now shift our focus on to the central proposition of Bentham's *ethical* system. His principle of utility went through several formulations and revisions. It is usually associated with the phrase 'the greatest happiness of the greatest number'; indeed, the first page of his first published work contained the statement: 'it is the greatest happiness of the greatest number that is the measure of right and wrong' (C/F 393). It is a curious fact that for more than forty years after 1776 the phrase did not reappear in his published works, but in the early 1820s he used it frequently, perhaps because it had a resonance which suited his purposes at that time as a radical publicist. The greatest happiness of the greatest number was described, for example, as 'the only right and proper end of sound action', and as the 'all-comprehensive object' of his *Constitutional Code* (B vii 582; CC i 18).

Later in the 1820s, however, he developed doubts about the phrase. He considered that 'the greatest happiness of the greatest number' was preferable to 'the greatest happiness of all', because conflicts of interest would always be liable to arise which might make it necessary for the happiness of some to be subordinated or sacrificed to that of others (B ix 6). On the other hand, he thought that the words 'the greatest number' might give the impression that the happiness of the majority was all that mattered, whereas in fact he believed that it would be possible for a minority to be oppressed by a majority in a way which caused more unhappiness to the former than it brought happiness to the latter, and which therefore reduced the overall happiness of the community. During the same decade he also

25

became dissatisfied with the phrase 'principle of utility', on the grounds that the term 'utility', which he had taken over from Hume and Helvétius, was not manifestly connected with the notion of maximizing happiness or pleasure. The label which eventually seemed to him more satisfactory, as a means of getting over both these difficulties, was 'the greatest happiness principle'.

As for fuller formulations or definitions of the principle, one of the most interesting—and also the last considered one which Bentham produced—is to be found in a pamphlet of 1831 entitled *Parliamentary Candidate's Proposed Declaration of Principles*. Here the 'only right and proper end of Government' is defined as

> the greatest happiness of the members of the community in question: the greatest happiness—of all of them, without exception, in so far as possible: the greatest happiness of the greatest number of them, on every occasion on which the nature of the case renders the provision of an equal quantity of happiness for every one of them impossible, by its being a matter of necessity, to make sacrifice of a portion of the happiness of a few, to the greater happiness of the rest.

This definition, to which attention has recently been drawn by Fred Rosen, is interesting partly for the light it throws on Bentham's views on equality.

One of the basic criticisms that have been levelled against Bentham's utilitarianism is that it sets up the maximization of *aggregate* happiness as the criterion of the rightness of actions, but does not include any intrinsic case for equality or fairness in the *distribution* of happiness. It has often been recognized that Bentham was aware of the phenomenon of diminishing marginal utility (of which more will be said in Chapter 3), and that this led him to regard equality in the distribution of the *means* of happiness (such as wealth) as conducive—other considerations apart—to the maximization of happiness in the aggregate. But a common assumption has been that his principle of utility did not prescribe that equality in the distribution of happiness *per se* was desirable; and substance is lent to this interpretation by a manuscript passage of 1789 in which Bentham wrote that, given one course of action which had the effect of providing each of ten persons with a single portion of happiness, and another course of action which had the effect of providing each of five persons with two equivalent portions, there would be no reason to regard one course as preferable to the other (UC clxx 114). However, it is clear from the 1831 definition of the greatest happiness principle that by then Bentham believed that the *optimal* goal included 'the provision of an equal quantity of happiness for every one', and thus that the maximization of happiness should be linked wherever possible to equality in its distribution.

Another feature of the formulation of 1831 that is worth noticing—though it does not distinguish it from many earlier definitions that Bentham had given—is the phrase 'the greatest happiness of the members of the community in question'. This is the definition of the object of government, and it underlines the fact that (as A. J. Ayer has said) the standpoint from which Bentham looked at questions of right and wrong was primarily a *social* one. The principle of utility or greatest happiness principle was chiefly intended as a precept addressed to legislators, to those responsible for the *management* of society; and he repeatedly said that the actions and policies of any such person should be judged by how far they were conducive to the happiness of his own community. He wrote in a manuscript of the 1780s, for example: 'The end of the conduct which a sovereign ought to observe relative to his own subjects—the end of the internal laws of a society,—ought to be the greatest happiness of the society concerned' (B ii 437). He was aware that other standpoints were possible. If, for example, one adopted the standpoint of a 'citizen of the world', as Bentham did in his writings on international law, the principle of utility could be extended to embrace the welfare of the human race as a whole. But he was mainly preoccupied throughout his life with legislation and other matters affecting a state's *internal* affairs, and for these purposes he regarded the appropriate criterion as being the happiness of the community.

Bentham

In assessing the behaviour of private individuals, Bentham customarily adopted the same social or community standpoint. He said that any action was 'conformable to the principle of utility' if its tendency was to increase rather than to diminish the happiness of the community—that is the happiness of those within the community, including the agent himself, whom the action was liable to affect (IPML 12–13, 285).

Relationship between the theory of human nature and the theory of ethics

This brings us to the question of how his principle of utility was connected—and how, indeed, it was reconcilable—with his psychology. A criticism that has often been levelled against him is that there was a fundamental incompatibility between the two. If one assumes, it is said, that every individual is bound to be motivated by the desire to promote his *own* happiness, how can one expect him to act in accordance with an ethical principle which lays down that the greatest happiness of the members of the community—or the greatest happiness of those whom his actions affect—is the object to be aimed at?

A portion of the answer lies in Bentham's belief that the individual's own happiness was a *part* of the happiness of the community, and the part of it that he was most likely to be able to promote effectively. It was one of Bentham's assumptions that each person—each responsible adult, at any rate—was normally the best judge of what his own happiness consisted in and of how it could best be pursued; it therefore seemed to him that the most important mechanism whereby happiness in the aggregate could be maximized was the basic drive of each individual to maximize his *own* happiness. A society which relied principally on this mechanism would be much happier than one in which each person concerned himself principally with the happiness of others. Bentham thought that Christian morality put too much stress on altruism, and that the precepts of Jesus, if taken literally, would be 'destructive of society' (BL 29806 472); for if each person ceased to give priority to providing for his own wants and safety, the human race would simply be unable to survive. In his view, self-regarding affection was essential for *diet*, though benevolence was a valuable addition for *dessert* (B x 511). He did not suggest that *anything* an individual did that was conducive to his own happiness was, in utilitarian terms, right. But he did believe that—provided it was subjected to suitable regulation—the operation of the principle of self-preference would accord, rather than conflict, with the principle of utility.

The other, and more fundamental, part of the answer to the question about the compatibility of Bentham's ethics with his psychology is that the principle of utility was not intended to be a principle by which ordinary individuals would be expected to regulate their moral conduct. It was intended, as we have already said, to be a precept addressed to legislators and others in positions of public trust. If one looked at the behaviour of ordinary individuals from the *social* standpoint—from the standpoint of the community and of those responsible for managing it—it made sense, in Bentham's view, to judge that behaviour as right or wrong according to how far it increased or diminished the general stock of happiness in the community. If, however, one considered matters from the standpoint of the individual, it made no sense to say that he *ought* to seek anything other than he was psychologically bound to seek. Although Bentham thought that every reasonable person would accept that the greatest happiness principle was the principle on which society as a whole ought to be *managed*, he did not expect each individual to aim at anything other than the maximization of his own happiness. He regarded as futile the sort of moralizing that consisted in telling people that they ought to behave differently from the ways in which they were disposed to behave; it was pointless to tell someone that he had a *duty* to do something unless it could be shown to be, or made to be, his *interest* to do it.

It will be apparent that Bentham was more concerned with modes of *influencing* behaviour than with passing judgements on it; and in so far as a person's conduct, assessed from the social point of view, was in conflict with the dictates of utility, the principal implication was not that the individual himself should be held personally responsible and culpable, but that the social arrangements and other factors that had conditioned his behaviour were at fault, and should as far as possible be adjusted so as to supply him with motives to behave otherwise. The essential purpose of Bentham's attempt to produce an exhaustive analysis of pains and pleasures, motives and sanctions, was to lay out before the legislator the factors that determined the conduct of human beings, and the possible means of influencing it.

What needed to be contrived was that people should pursue their own happiness in ways that were either innocuous, or actually conducive, to the happiness of others; and the basic means available to the legislator for achieving this were punishments and rewards (or threats of punishment and offers of reward). Rewards were the less important instrument of the two, being principally useful for obtaining certain services to the public. So far as the people at large were concerned, punishments were the legislator's chief resource. His aim in employing these was, through the infliction and (chiefly) the threat of pain, to provide people with motives for abstaining from socially harmful behaviour: to deter them, in other words, from pursuing their own happiness through actions which would have the effect of reducing the stock of happiness in the community.

Bentham also considered that there was a second, subsidiary mode in which the legislator could influence conduct: through 'indirect' legislation. This included measures designed to *prevent* crime by increasing the likelihood that criminals would be detected and convicted. It also included measures aimed at 'adjusting the propensities of men to the standard of utility' (UC lxxxvii 27). In his unfinished essay on indirect legislation written in the 1780s, he mooted various relatively 'oblique' methods which governments could use, or consider using, to influence people's inclinations in ways that were conducive to the general happiness. These methods (discussed further in Chapter 6) included forms of propaganda and public instruction intended to strengthen and direct the impact of the 'moral or popular sanction'—that is, to influence the general climate of opinion and hence, via people's 'love of reputation', the ways in which they behaved.

In addition to legislation and indirect legislation, there was a third mode of influencing behaviour which Bentham discussed: what he called in his *Introduction to the Principles* 'private ethics', and in his later years 'private deontology'. This was not considered by him as a branch or aspect of legislation. He regarded the 'deontologist' as having a separate role from that of the legislator, and as operating from a different standpoint: a standpoint that was *personal* rather than social. Some commentators have inferred from the term 'private ethics' that what Bentham was talking about was a mode of *judging* private behaviour. In fact, the deontologist or exponent of private ethics was not envisaged as a judge or arbiter of morals, but as a teacher; his role was to instruct the individual how to maximize his *own* happiness. He could not take as the direct objective of his teaching the maximization of the *general* happiness, for he was not—as the legislator was—in a position to *create* motives for influencing behaviour in that direction. He had to operate with 'such motives as offer of themselves' (IPML 293)—that is, with whatever motives arose or could be educed from the personal nature and situation of the individuals he was teaching; and, given Bentham's views on psychology, he could only cause those individuals to consult the happiness of others to the extent that he could show them that they would maximize their own happiness by doing so.

However, although the deontologist operated from a different standpoint from that of the legislator, Bentham thought that in effect his work could contribute significantly to the legislator's objective of maximizing the happiness of the community. He divided the subject-matter of practical deontology into two branches: that of 'self-regarding prudence', which concerned the means whereby a man could procure happiness for himself independently of his relations with other people, and that of 'extra-regarding prudence', which concerned the area of behaviour in which his happiness *was* affected by his conduct in relation to others. By teaching individuals how to maximize their own long-term happiness in the 'purely self-

31

regarding' area of conduct, the deontologist would be helping incidentally to increase *aggregate* happiness; and his teaching of 'extra-regarding prudence' would have the same effect in a compound fashion by showing the many different ways in which a man's long-term happiness was best promoted by 'an intermediate regard shown in practice for the happiness of others' (D 123).

A possible question that Bentham anticipated was how it could be considered necessary to teach people to maximize their own happiness when it had been laid down as a general rule that each person was the best judge of his own happiness and of how to promote it. His answer was that although the rule was 'in no inconsiderable part solid' it did admit of certain exceptions. He considered that in both the self-regarding and the extra-regarding areas of behaviour the individual might not always take, spontaneously, as comprehensive and far-sighted a view of the possible consequences of his actions as the expert deontologist might be able to take. While each individual was certainly the best judge of the *value* to himself of each pleasure and pain, what the deontologist could do was to bring to his attention potential pleasures and pains which might be overlooked but needed to be taken into account.

It will be apparent that in Bentham's discussion of private ethics (as in his treatment of public policy) there was a strong emphasis on calculation. He went so far as to suggest in the *Deontology* that acts of beneficence that were of no immediate advantage to the agent might be regarded as deposits paid into a savings bank or General Good-will Fund, from which the agent might expect to draw benefits in due course. Also, in opposition to those moralists whose teaching involved a continuous demand for painful sacrifices, Bentham argued that *economy* of sacrifice should be recommended; for although it might often be desirable to sacrifice a lesser quantity of happiness for the sake of obtaining a greater quantity, it was in general true that the less happiness was sacrificed the larger would be the amount remaining.

Comparison with other ethical systems

Earlier in this chapter, we observed that Bentham did not claim that the validity of his greatest happiness principle was something that could be logically demonstrated. He did think, however, that there were a number of considerations that would make the principle acceptable and attractive to reasonable men. Having described the principle itself and how he envisaged it as operating, let us conclude the chapter by looking at the reasons he gave for regarding his own moral system as preferable to others. Many of his arguments were concerned with exposing the defects and inferiority of other systems, or with showing that when examined closely they turned out to be disguised versions or perversions of the one he was upholding. He maintained in the second chapter of the *Introduction to the Principles* that all systems which rejected the principle of utility could be classified as involving adherence to one or other of two rival principles: the principle of asceticism, and the principle of sympathy and antipathy— which he later renamed the principle of caprice, and later still referred to as the principle of sentimentalism or ipsedixitism.

The principle of asceticism he defined as the principle which judged actions right in so far as they produced pain and wrong in so far as they produced pleasure. While recognizing that this principle had never been consistently maintained and pursued, he thought that some moralists and religious devotees did teach, or had taught, that pleasure was something to be distrusted and even eschewed and that suffering was a source of merit. Many such people, he believed, were unconsciously applying—or misapplying—the principle of utility in their own fashion. Either they were recommending ascetic behaviour on the supposition that this was the way to earn God's approval and thus to maximize one's happiness in the world to come; or, having perceived that indulgence in some pleasures was inclined to produce more than equivalent pains in *this* world, they had rushed on to the unfounded conclusion that 'every thing that offered itself under the name of pleasure' should be regarded as wrong. As for the possibility that the principle of

Bentham

asceticism could be deliberately and consistently applied, Bentham said that if it were acted upon by any significant number of people the world would be immediately converted into a hell.

The moral systems which he lumped together as depending on the principle of sympathy and antipathy were all those which he regarded as reducible in the last resort to the subjective judgements or feelings of the people who enunciated them. According to these moralists, the test of whether actions were right or wrong was whether or not they conformed to the dictates of the law of nature, or right reason, or the moral sense, or any of a number of similar concepts or phrases. But how could one tell what the dictates of, for example, the law of nature were? No two people were likely to agree in every particular about this; and the ultimate ground for deciding what the law of nature decreed was nothing more than one man's opinion or sentiment against another's. This was true, at least, unless a moralist tried to justify the positions he took up by making some kind of appeal to utility, thereby conceding in effect that his criterion was not an independent and self-sufficient one and that the principle of utility was the ultimate arbiter.

Bentham considered that the dictates of the principle of sympathy and antipathy (unlike those of the principle of asceticism) did often coincide with those of the principle of utility, for the various adherents of the former principle tended to be more or less unconsciously influenced, in their moral likes and dislikes, by considerations of what was beneficial and what was mischievous. But in so far as they *avoided* an appeal to utility, their moral discourse was mere assertion or 'ipsedixitism'. They were saying that actions were right or wrong—should be approved or disapproved—according to whether or not they conformed to (say) the law of nature; and for determining what constituted the law of nature they offered no essential grounds beyond their own feelings of approval or disapproval. Appeals to *authority* did not get round the problem, for as there was no universally agreed text of the law of nature each person had to choose, on all doubtful points, which

34

authorities to invoke. For similar reasons, appeals to divine law or the 'Law of Revelation' were equally subjective and inconclusive, there being so many different ways in which the scriptures could be interpreted (C/F 10–28).

Bentham also put forward more positive arguments to support the view that the principle of utility was preferable to its rivals. Perhaps the most important argument was that his principle did make it possible to evaluate human behaviour in ways that were not merely subjective:

> What one expects to find in a principle is something that points out some external consideration, as a means of warranting and guiding the internal sentiments of approbation and disapprobation: this expectation is but ill fulfilled by a proposition, which does neither more nor less than hold up each of those sentiments as a ground and standard of itself. (IPML 25)

The principle of utility, by laying down that actions should be judged by reference to their effects in terms of pleasure and pain, did require the application of an 'external' standard, and thus made moral questions depend on reasoned argument instead of mere sentiment and assertion. By the use of this principle, he wrote in a work of the mid-1790s, 'the question is put, as every political and moral question ought to be, upon the issue of fact; and mankind are directed into the only true track of investigation which can afford instruction or hope of rational argument, the track of experiment and observation' (B ii 495).

A related point was that Bentham's system provided scope for calculations of extent and proportion. As he wrote in 1820: 'In ethics, utility depends altogether on proportions; which *ipse-dixitism* . . . neglects' (B x 518). According to the principle of utility as defined in the *Introduction to the Principles* (13), the approval or disapproval annexed to any action should be determined by, and *proportioned to*, the tendency it was conceived to have to augment or diminish the happiness of the community; whereas according to the principle of sympathy and antipathy there was no way of judging to what extent an action was right or wrong except by how strongly one approved or disapproved of it. A further argument that he used was that moral systems other than his own provided *definitions* of what conduct was right, but could not provide any substantial answer to the question of what *motives* anyone had to act accordingly. His own system, however, provided the means of explaining, in terms of pleasure and pain, not only how people ought to behave, but how they did behave and could be made to behave; and it was able to show that people had many motives, and could be supplied with others, for conforming their behaviour to the dictates of utility.

A final point worth mentioning, which Bentham made in his *Deontology* (122), was that his own ethical system would surely be more *attractive* than those of 'gloomier' moralists, because it did not call for self-denial for its own sake but invested the subject of morals with a 'light and pleasant hue'. It has to be said, however, that there were people who found his views on psychology and private ethics far from attractive. Thomas Carlyle was thinking of Bentham when he criticized those sages who devoted themselves to 'counting-up and estimating men's motives', and who attempted 'by curious checking and balancing, and other adjustments of profit and loss, to guide them to their true advantage'; for them good conduct was a matter of prudence and 'cunning love of self' rather than a matter of virtue, and they ignored the vital and spiritual elements, 'the inward and primary powers of man', which were the true sources of human worth and happiness (ER xlvi 348, xlix 447–52). Also, John Stuart Mill considered that Bentham had overstressed the predominance of self-regarding interest in human motivation, and had ignored the extent to which people could be influenced by a sense of rectitude or by a desire for spiritual perfection as an end in itself. A function of ethics, he said, should be to inspire people with a love, and with a belief in the possibility, of virtue, whereas Bentham's analysis of human behaviour was more likely to induce fatalism and to legitimize self-seeking. Bentham's response might have been that a relatively small proportion of mankind would be capable of responding, at least in a sustained fashion, to a moral teaching that relied on appeals to each person's better self. His view of human nature was not a sanguine one, a favourite quotation of his being a remark in Helvétius's *De l'esprit*: 'To love one's fellow-men, one must not expect much of them' (D 189 n).

3 Language and method

William Hazlitt, in a clever and stylish essay on Bentham published in 1824, made a number of provocative points, one of which was that the subject of the essay could 'not be looked upon in the light of a discoverer in legislation or morals'. It is clear, however, that Bentham did think of himself as a discoverer or inventor, and there are several respects in which his claims to be so regarded are worth considering.

At the most practical level (to which Hazlitt of course was not referring), Bentham shared his brother's interest in *mechanical* invention, though his projects at this level were mostly abortive. One finds him writing at length to the Home Office in 1793 proposing that the various government departments should be linked by a network of 'conversation-tubes'; a few years later he tried with the help of Peter Mark Roget (then a young scientist, later compiler of the *Thesaurus*) to construct a 'Frigidarium' or ice-house in which perishable foods could be kept for a substantial time without decay or loss of flavour; and at the same period he was trying to interest the Bank of England in a printing technique that would produce an unforgeable banknote. The most famous joint invention of the Bentham brothers was the Panopticon, which has been described by an architectural historian, Robin Evans, as a 'vividly imaginative' fusion of architectural form with social purpose.

But what about invention at the more theoretical level which Hazlitt had in mind? It is true that, as Hazlitt went on to say in his essay, there was nothing very original about the principle of utility. Although Bentham invented the term 'utilitarian', he had many precursors in the tradition of moral philosophy to which that label can be retrospectively applied. He himself was very frank, indeed almost repetitious, in acknowledging his intellectual debts, and he wrote around 1780 that the principle he was taking for the groundwork of his intended Pannomion was far from being a new one. He added, however: 'What was wanting was not sagacity to discover it, but only resolution to pursue it' (UC xxvii 100). He certainly thought that in his mode of *applying* the principle he was breaking new ground. He neatly distinguished his own approach in this respect from that of Hume when he said in a letter to Dumont in 1822 that Hume had used the principle 'to *account* for that which is—I to shew what *ought to be*' (Dm. 33/I 167). Hume, in other words, had confined himself to showing that the established rules or conventions of morality and justice were ultimately founded on their usefulness to mankind. Helvétius had gone further, Bentham thought, in that in *De l'esprit* 'a commencement was made of the application of the principle of utility to practical uses' (D 290). But it was he himself who had employed it *systematically* as an instrument of reform and innovation.

Systematic application is not the same thing as discovery. But Bentham wrote in his *Chrestomathia* (166), the work on education which he published in 1816, that among the objects, as well as the instruments, of invention and discovery was *method*; and it was in virtue of his methodology as a writer on law and government that he was most apt to claim originality. John Stuart Mill strongly supported his claim in this respect. He wrote that Bentham had 'introduced into morals and politics those habits of thought and modes of investigation, which are essential to the idea of science. . . . It was not his opinions, . . . but his method, that constituted the novelty and value of what he did.'

Linguistic precision and neutrality

The most basic thing which Bentham thought in need of reform if the science of legislation was to advance was language, which he associated closely with logic. He was acutely conscious of the scope for ambiguity and confusion which arose from the wealth of synonyms which existed and from the variety of meanings which a single word might have; and he was appalled by the fact that many writers, even in fields where linguistic precision was vital, seemed unaware of the need for careful definition and consistency in the use of terms. A prime illustration of this negligence, in his opinion, was the French Declaration of the Rights of Man, which he attacked in a work called 'Anarchical Fallacies' written in the mid-1790s. He described it as

> a perpetual vein of nonsense, flowing from a perpetual abuse of words,—words having a variety of meanings, where words with single meanings were equally at hand,—the same words used in a variety of meanings on the same page,—. . . the same inaccuracy, the same inattention in the penning of this cluster of truths on which the fate of nations was to hang, as if it had been an oriental tale, or an allegory for a magazine. (B ii 497)

It was not only the looseness of the phraseology that he objected to in this document. He also considered that its language was emotive and rhetorical. Words could be used, he maintained, either to convey information, or for the purpose of 'excitation' (or for both purposes at once). So far as the communication of information alone was concerned, there was little need to worry about the possibility that the powers of language might be dangerously misused. But where language was employed to excite the passions one should always be on one's guard, for passion was the 'everlasting enemy' of reason and sound judgement (B viii 301). The modes of communication he particularly distrusted were rhetoric and poetry, which he called the two branches of the art of misrepresentation (UC x 96). Poetry, he wrote, was incompatible with truth and exactitude: the poet 'must see everything through coloured media, and strive to make everyone else do the same'; rhetoric he described as 'the art of misdirecting the judgment by agitating and inflaming the passions' (B ii 253–4, x 510).

A more subtle aspect of the emotiveness of language was the element of prejudice or value judgement, sometimes more or less concealed, that was inherent in a great number of words. In his *Defence of Usury* he argued that a major cause of the continued existence of the Usury Laws (which imposed legal restraints on the rate of interest) was the word 'usury' itself, with its extortionate and semitic associations; this was the main source, he wrote, of 'the hold which the opinion I am combating has obtained on the imaginations and passions of mankind' (B iii 3). Another work of his, *A Table of the Springs of Action*, was a sustained examination of the bias inherent in words. In his opinion no motive should be regarded as good or bad in itself. The goodness or badness of an action depended on the consequences that flowed from it in the context in which it was performed. (Even the motive of benevolence could have ill effects if one's sympathies led one to promote the happiness or advantage of a particular individual or group at the cost of greater unhappiness or disadvantage to others.) Yet many of the names attached to motives carried connotations of approval or disapproval; and in his *Table* Bentham listed under the different motives the 'neutral', 'eulogistic', and 'dyslogistic' names commonly given to them. Thus for the motive corresponding to 'pecuniary interest' there were eulogistic names such as 'frugality' and 'thrift', and a range of dyslogistic ones such as 'parsimony', 'cupidity', 'avarice'. For the motive called 'sexual desire', he could think of no eulogistic names but plenty of dyslogistic ones: 'lust', 'lechery', 'lewdness', etc.

The one-sidedness of the latter example is worth pausing over. Sex, in Bentham's opinion, was a major source of pleasure, and as such should be regarded as presumptively good. He wrote of the sexual act in a manuscript of 1816: 'Unless and until effects not only noxious but noxious in a preponderant degree can be shewn to flow from it, the operation can not but be acknowledged to be not simply innoxious but positively beneficial; for unless attended with pleasure it never is performed' (UC lxxiv 62). In a much earlier manuscript he had gone so far as to say that sex was the 'highest enjoyment' that nature had bestowed upon man (UC lxxiv 8). And yet—as a result, in his view, of the application of the 'principle of asceticism' by a church which derived its attitudes on these matters largely from St Paul—sex had come to be plastered with pejorative labels and associated with shame and impurity. By contrast, he pointed to the eulogistic slant of the word 'honour', which was prominent in his list of motives corresponding to the 'pleasures of reputation'. Action motivated by a sense of honour was generally assumed to be commendable; and often, indeed, it was. Yet how frequently had the use of the word, in relation to national and international concerns, been a factor contributing to war, and thus to '*homicide*, *depredation*, and *destruction*—human suffering in all manner of shapes upon the largest scale'. And how much better it would have been if the distrust with which people had been taught to regard the pursuit of sexual pleasure had been directed towards the pursuit of such empty and even pernicious objectives as national honour and dignity (B iv 438; D 233).

His concern that people should pay close attention to the substance of the terms they used and thereby emancipate themselves from the 'tyranny of sounds' (B iii 21) was particularly apparent, as one would expect, in his treatment of the vocabulary of law and politics. In these fields, he wrote, there was 'a numerous tribe of words, of which . . . the meaning had been floating in the clouds, and blown about by every blast of doctrine' (B iii 286). Examples he gave included the words 'obligation' and 'right'; and it was to clarify his views on how such terms *ought* to be used that he developed his theory of 'fictions'.

Fictitious entities

He maintained that all nouns could be divided into two classes: the names of real entities and the names of fictitious entities. A real entity was something of whose existence people had an immediate consciousness and conviction: material objects, sensory perceptions, and ideas existing in people's minds as a result of the recollection and consideration of such perceptions. He appreciated that some might find it hard to accept that perceptions and ideas should be regarded as real entities. But he said that our consciousness of the reality of these things is even more direct than our knowledge of the reality of corporeal objects, whose existence we only infer from the evidence of our senses. Pleasures and pains, together with 'neutral' sensations, were treated by Bentham as the most basic, because the most immediately perceptible, of real entities.

A fictitious entity was something that was *spoken of* as if it really existed, in that it was denoted grammatically (like a real entity) by a noun-substantive; but in fact existence was not meant to be ascribed to it. The names of fictitious entities were linguistic constructions, some with a physical application and some with a 'psychical' one (that is, applying to mental phenomena). In the former category were nouns classifiable under the headings of motion, quantity, quality, form, and relation. In the latter category were, first, what he called 'ontological' fictitious entities: those relating to being and existence, such as 'certainty' and 'impossibility'. Second, there were what he called (in the broadest sense of the word) 'ethical' fictitious entities: those relating to human conduct, including political and legal concepts such as 'obligation', 'right', 'power', etc. (B viii 263–4; Chr. 259 n). Bentham realized that the term 'fictitious entities' might be thought to imply disapproval—to imply that the use of such modes of speech ought to be avoided. He himself, indeed, often used the term 'fiction' (as we shall see in Chapter 4) to describe devices which he regarded as mendacious and delusive. However, what he called 'the logical species of fiction' was essential to human discourse: essential, at any rate, to 'language in any form superior to that of the language of the brute creation' (B viii 198–9).

The trouble with fictitious entities—and notably those of the political or legal variety—was that they were very apt to give rise to confusion. For one thing, they tended to become what we should now call 'reified'. People tended to assume that these verbal constructs really existed as things in themselves, and the terms were used in an unthinking way as if their content was palpable and unproblematic, when in fact people had little idea of what they signified. Bentham wrote in 1819: '*Give us our rights*, say the thousands and the millions. . . . Yet, of all who say so, not one perhaps can say, not one perhaps ever conceived clearly, what it is he thus calls for—what sort of a thing *a right* is' (B iii 594 n). He considered that his distinction

43

between real and fictitious entities helped, in a useful and novel way, to draw attention to those terms which were most in need of exposition. He also thought that he had invented a *method* of expounding them which enabled one to tell which fictitious entities were meaningful and therefore legitimate and which were not.

The traditional Aristotelian method of definition was called *definitio per genus et differentiam*, whereby one identified an object first by indicating the genus or class to which it belonged, and then by indicating the characteristic quality which distinguished it from other species or members of the same class. Where fictitious entities were concerned, Bentham argued, this method was frequently inapplicable, for in the case of many of them there was no superior genus to which they could be said to belong. This was true, for example, of a 'right', which was not a species of anything. One could say that a 'right' was a kind of 'power'; but then one could also say that a 'power' was a kind of 'right'. If one tried to define a fictitious entity by referring to another fictitious entity which was also in need of definition, one would get no further forward (C/F 495 n; D 78). The way out of this impasse was the method he called 'paraphrasis'. What this involved was the formulation of two parallel propositions: in the first, the name of the fictitious entity needing to be expounded was the leading term; in the second, the same import was expressed, but the term at the crux of the proposition was the name of a real entity instead of that of a fictitious one. Bentham considered that fictitious entities were only acceptable when they could be expounded in this way by reference to real entities. In *Of Laws in General* (251) he described fictitious legal entities as 'a sort of paper currency: if we know how at any time to change them and get sterling in their room, it is well: if not, . . . we possess nothing but sophistry and nonsense'.

The terms to which he applied his method most directly and explicitly were 'obligations' (or 'duties') and 'rights'. To say that a person was 'under an obligation' to do something was only meaningful, he claimed, if one could translate this into a statement that in the event of his not doing it he was liable to

experience a *sensation* in the form of a pain or loss of pleasure.
Such pains might flow from any of the 'sanctions' enumerated
by Bentham in his analysis of motivation. In the case of a *moral*
obligation, for example, the pains liable to be suffered would
derive from the popular or moral sanction: in other words,
would take the form of 'various mortifications resulting from
the ill-will of . . . the community in general' or of such
members of the community as the individual concerned
happened to be connected with. In the case of a legal obligation, the pains to be anticipated were of course the penalties
ordained by the law.

As for *rights*, Bentham thought that for these to have any
substance they had to depend on *obligations*, and that in order
to be related to real entities they needed to be expounded in
terms of obligations in the first place, and thence in terms of
pains. To say that a person had a right thus meant that another
person was under an obligation to do something—or to refrain
from doing something—affecting him, and that this other person was liable to incur pain by failing to conform to the
obligation in question. If, without reference to pain or punishment, one told a person that he had a duty to act in a particular
way, one was simply saying that one thought he *ought* to act
in this way; and if, similarly, one told a person that he had a
right to something, one was simply expressing the opinion that
he *ought* to have it. The use of the terms 'duty' and 'right' in
this disembodied fashion—like the use of the terms 'natural
law' and 'right reason' discussed in Chapter 2—was mere
ipsedixitism, the mere assertion of 'internal sentiment' (B viii
247; C/F 495–6 n).

C. K. Ogden (co-author with I. A. Richards of *The Meaning
of Meaning*), who 'rediscovered' Bentham's work on language
and logic during the inter-war period, said that in this area he
was almost without predecessors and entirely without col-
laborators. There had been earlier writers, of course, who were
deeply interested in the analysis of words. For instance, one of
the books of Locke's *Essay concerning Human Understanding*
had been devoted to this subject, and a chapter of Helvétius's
De l'esprit had been called 'The abuse of language'. Also,

Bentham

Bentham acknowledged a debt to d'Alembert in regard to the concept of fictitious entities, and he expressed qualified admiration for the philological work of his own contemporary John Horne Tooke, who was concerned to dispel the mystery and obscurity of abstract terms by showing how they were derived from words signifying very ordinary operations and sensations. But there is no doubt that Bentham's work in this field was original; and it is also clear that he attached much more importance to it than one would guess from the occasional footnotes and appendices which were all he devoted to it in the works published in his own lifetime. Two other aspects of his methodology which he regarded as important, and which similarly underlay and informed his general approach to legislation, will be briefly discussed in the remainder of this chapter: classification and quantification.

Classification

Bentham was interested, as we have seen, in the sciences, and the ones which seemed most relevant and helpful to him as a *social* scientist were those such as medicine and botany in which classification played a major part. He said that from the point of view of method he had learnt more from books relating to these fields than he had from law books. One work which made an impression on him was William Cullen's *Nosology*, a classification of diseases according to their genera and species, first published in 1769, and he was also impressed by the systematic classification of plants carried out in the mid-eighteenth century by the Swedish naturalist Carl Linnaeus. Such works led him to ask why a similar degree of order could not be introduced into the field of legislation, and they helped to inspire the 'division of offences' which formed a large part of the *Introduction to the Principles* and which he described as a 'nosology of the body politic' (C vii 27).

The specific mode of analysis he adopted was the one which had been used by the eighteenth-century grammarian James Harris and the sixteenth-century French humanist Peter

Ramus: the method of 'bipartition' or 'bifurcate division'. According to this method, a logical whole was analysed or broken down into its component parts through a series of dichotomies. At each stage, a 'superior' class of objects or concepts was divided into two mutually exclusive sub-classes, distinguished from each other by a characteristic which the members of one sub-class possessed and those of the other did not. It was vital that at each stage the division should be into two sub-classes and no more, partly because the mind was only capable of comparing two things at any one moment, and partly because it was only by this means that one could be certain that each partition was exhaustive in the sense of extending to every member of the class being divided. The process of division and sub-division could be carried on for as long as the distinctions drawn continued to be useful.

One problem which the method raised was that of nomenclature. Ideally, at each bipartition each of the two sub-classes identified should be given a name which indicated both what the two sub-classes had in common (that is, their joint membership of the superior class) *and* what distinguished each from the other. But for names which could convey the subtleties involved, suitable terms in common use were often hard to find, and Bentham had to decide how far he would go in inventing new ones. In the *Introduction to the Principles* (188 n, 215 n) he said that if one tried to introduce an entirely new set of terms one could be sure of not being understood; all one could realistically do was to invent a new term occasionally when it seemed absolutely necessary, and otherwise to 'patch up' the language available. But when he came to compile for his *Chrestomathia* an encyclopaedic table of the various branches of knowledge, analysed in the bifurcate mode, he produced an amazing array of new terms derived from Greek. It should be noted in passing that in the course of his life he did invent some valuable new words: international, maximize and minimize, codify and codification. But he was optimistic in imagining that people would adopt for purposes of education the neologisms of his encylopaedic table, where one finds, for example, physiurgic somatology (alias natural

47

history) being divided into uranoscopic physiurgics (astronomy) and epigeoscopic physiurgics (knowledge of things upon the earth).

Whatever difficulties there were about nomenclature, Bentham attached great value to the method of bipartition, and went so far as to say in the *Introduction in the Principles* (196 n): 'If there be anything new and original in this work, it is to the exhaustive method so often aimed at that I am indebted for it.' It was certainly novel as applied to the field of legislation, and one can see why, as a believer in codification, Bentham found it so attractive. He thought that by means of it he could produce a systematic and exhaustive catalogue of offences or crimes, which would in turn provide the basis for an ordered and comprehensive code of penal law. The mode of presentation would enable the legislator to combine a general conspectus or 'panoptic' view of the subject with a clear understanding of its detailed ramifications and their interrelationships. The arrangement was also a 'natural' rather than a 'technical' one. Instead of being classed in terms of obscure categories and denominations such as 'misprisions, contempts, felonies, praemunires', which had grown up adventitiously within a particular legal system, offences were defined and classified in accordance with the ways in which they respectively damaged the happiness of the community. (The classification began with a division into offences against assignable individuals and offences against unassignable individuals. The first class was then divided into 'private extraregarding' offences, against assignable individuals other than the offender, and 'self-regarding' offences, detrimental to the offender himself. The second class was divided into 'public' offences, against the community as a whole, and 'semi-public' offences, against a neighbourhood or class of people. The process of bipartition proceeded from there.) In such an arrangement, Bentham claimed, there was no place in which an action that was *not* damaging to the community could be classed as an offence, whereas a technical arrangement, he wrote, 'is a sink that with equal facility will swallow any garbage that is thrown into it'. A further great advantage of his natural arrangement was that, being based on a principle that was applicable to man in general, it was not tied to the conditions of any particular community: it would 'serve alike for the jurisprudence of all nations' (IPML 272–4; C/F 415–18).

Quantification

Some of Bentham's contemporaries found his classifications (as he knew they would) distinctly tiresome, and thought that he was obsessed with making lists; and one objection was that these lists contained no guidance as to how important or trivial the various items were. Hazlitt said that Bentham's method produced something more like an inventory than a valuation, and the Scottish lawyer Francis Jeffrey wrote in a review of the *Traités de législation* in the *Edinburgh Review* (iv 15) that his 'endless tables and divisions' provided no means of 'measuring or comparing utilities'. In the theory of punishments which corresponded to his treatment of offences, however, Bentham *was* concerned with questions of quantity: with achieving 'economy' of punishment by calculating the minimum amount of pain that had to be inflicted to provide effective deterrence. Also, in general, the notion that conduct could be influenced by the manipulation of punishments and rewards, pains and pleasures, and the belief that the maximization of happiness should be the end of government, implied that serious thought should be given to the question of how happiness could be measured.

While he did not often use the term 'welfare', Bentham did suggest in the *Deontology* (130) that the term 'well-being' might be more suitable than 'happiness' to denote the overall condition which needed to be measured. 'Happiness', he said, seemed to leave pains out of the account, and also seemed to indicate a degree and intensity of enjoyment that relatively few people were able to attain. 'Well-being' was a better word for designating 'the *difference* in *value* between the sum of the pleasures of all sorts and the sum of the pains of all sorts' which a man experienced in a given period of time.

But what were pleasures and pains and how could they be

measured? As we have seen in considering Bentham's theory of
motivation, he recognized that there was a great variety of
pleasures by which people could be motivated. Everything a
person did, according to him—every action, at least, that was
the outcome of *will*—was motivated by a desire for some
pleasure or an aversion to some pain; and the pleasures listed
in *A Table of the Springs of Action* included those of the palate,
those of power, those of amity, those of revenge. Bentham
explicitly admitted that exact comparisons between different
kinds of pleasure, as experienced by different people with different sensibilities, were difficult if not impossible to make,
and that attempts to aggregate these various pleasures were
bound to be artificial. He went so far as to write in an undated
manuscript passage: ' 'Tis in vain to talk of adding quantities
which after the addition will continue distinct as they were
before, one man's happiness will never be another man's happiness: a gain to one man is no gain to another: you might as well
pretend to add 20 apples to 20 pears.' But he went on to say that
from the point of view of the legislator or policy-maker some
assumptions about the basic homogeneity of people's
preferences or utilities had to be made: 'This addibility of the
happiness of different subjects, however when considered
rigorously it may appear fictitious, is a postulatum without the
allowance of which all political reasonings are at a stand' (UC
xiv 3).

The notion of 'addibility' implied, of course, that the happiness, the pleasures and pains, of individuals *could* in some
sense be measured. The best-known passage in which he confronted the question of how this could be done was the short
chapter he devoted to it in the *Introduction to the Principles*;
but he also tackled the subject at a somewhat more searching
level in a manuscript of the late 1770s, and he returned to it
later in a section of his *Codification Proposal* of 1822 (UC
xxvii 29–40; B iv 540–3). In these places he expounded his
idea—which he later included in 1814 in a list of his own
'instruments of invention and discovery', though he acknowledged that the first hint of it had been derived from Beccaria
(B iii 286)—that there were certain 'dimensions' of value in terms

of which a 'lot' of pleasure or pain could be assessed.

The magnitude of a pleasure (or pain), considered as experienced by a single person, was basically determined by its *intensity*, and by its *duration*. In regard to a future pleasure, a pleasure in prospect, two other factors had to be taken into account: the degree of its *propinquity* or remoteness, and the degree of *certainty* with which it could be expected. Bentham explained these last two dimensions by treating pleasure as analogous to money. A promise of a sum of money payable in ten years' time would be regarded at the present moment as having only a proportion of its eventual value, that proportion depending on the rate of discount; and if one added an element of uncertainty, its present value would be reduced further, in proportion to the risk of the promise not being eventually honoured. To arrive at the *overall* value of a future pleasure, one should multiply together the figures representing the four different dimensions, intensity, duration, propinquity, and certainty (the latter pair of dimensions being represented by fractions). In the case of a pleasure that was to be enjoyed by more than one person, one needed to bring in a fifth dimension and multiplier: the *extent* of the pleasure, represented by the number of people who would experience it.

Of these five dimensions, Bentham considered that the last four were all more or less quantifiable, but he had doubts about the first. In the manuscript of the 1770s he suggested that the basic unit of intensity might be defined as 'the degree of intensity possessed by that pleasure which is the faintest of any that can be distinguished to be pleasure'—thereby anticipating the concept of the *'minimum sensibile'* which F. Y. Edgeworth proposed a hundred years later as the unit for measuring pleasure and pain. In his *Codification Proposal*, however, Bentham conceded that the dimension of intensity was 'not susceptible of precise expression: it *not* being susceptible of measurement'.

Another question that was explored in the manuscript was how far pleasures in general might be measurable in terms of money. At this stage he thought that although not all pleasures were purchasable it might be possible to value those that were

not through comparison with those that were: if, for example,
'between two pleasures, the one produced by the possession of
money, the other not, a man had as lief enjoy the one as the
other, such pleasures are to be reputed equal'. He recognized
that money itself might have a differing value for people in differing circumstances, but money nevertheless seemed to him
'the only common measure the nature of things affords'; those
who were not satisfied with the accuracy of this gauge must
either find another that was more accurate, or give up hope of
making quantitative judgements in morals and politics.

Subsequently, however, he modified this view as a result of
his increased awareness of the diminishing marginal utility of
money. His perception of this phenomenon was not something
that he included among his 'discoveries', but it can be seen in
retrospect as one of his most impressive insights; for although
some of his contemporaries, such as the theistic utilitarian
William Paley, showed a vague awareness of it, none of them
identified it as clearly as Bentham did. He did not get to the
stage of giving it a name, but the most explicit passage he wrote
about it was in a set of manuscripts that was published after his
death under the title 'Pannomial Fragments'. He said here:

> The effect of wealth in the production of happiness goes on
> diminishing, as the quantity by which the wealth of one man
> exceeds that of another goes on increasing: in other words,
> the quantity of happiness produced by a particle of wealth
> (each particle being of the same magnitude) will be less and
> less at every particle. (B iii 229)

And he went on to say that the wealthier a man was, the less
subtraction would be made from his happiness by the subtraction of a given particle of wealth.

A shorter but similar exposition was published in his lifetime
in the *Codification Proposal*. In that work, having indicated
that diminishing marginal utility was a major obstacle to the
use of money as a measure of hedonic value, he went on to
express his general conclusions about 'the application . . . of
arithmetic to questions of utility'. He admitted that it was not
possible to achieve the same degree of quantitative precision in

morals and politics as was attainable in some other fields. None the less, he said, it was important that attention should be paid to questions of quantity and proportion on all occasions. However far this approach might fall short of perfect precision, 'at any rate, in every rational and candid eye, unspeakable will be the advantage it will have over every form of argumentation in which every idea is afloat, no degree of precision being ever attained because none is ever so much as aimed at' (B iv 542). In the end his claims about quantification were quite cautious, but he did raise, more sharply than any of his contemporaries, many of the questions relating to it which have continued to exercise psychologists, economists, and others. One commentator, emphasizing the limitations of Bentham's so-called calculus, said that he came nearer to being the Linnaeus than the Newton of the moral world. Another, however, has written that his concern with measurement marked 'the crucial transition from hedonistic philosophy to modern social science'.

4 Codification versus common law

Bentham wrote in 1796: 'If one branch of knowledge be in its nature more interesting than another, it should be this of Law, on the breath of which personal security, life, property, reputation, condition in life, everything that can bear the name of interest depends' (UC cliii 119). Law was the essential source of social order and cohesion, and thus of individual security. But he did not believe that the legal systems of his own time, including the English one, provided these benefits nearly as effectively as they should have done. Much of his time, especially in the 1770s, was devoted to demonstrating the deficiencies of the English system in these respects. Meanwhile he was formulating his own ideal alternative, a system in which all law emanated from, or was endorsed by, a sovereign lawgiver or legislative body committed to the principle of utility.

In the late eighteenth century English law was a combination of common law and statute law. The volume of law enacted by Parliament was increasing rapidly, but the common law was still the predominant element, and most English lawyers regarded it as intrinsically superior to statute. Indeed, one of William Blackstone's chief concerns in his *Commentaries on the Laws of England* was to emphasize the virtues of common law and to warn against the expansion of parliamentary legislation. As he and others saw it, the common law had been built up over the centuries, and the rules and practices it embodied were the outcome of the wisdom and experience of many generations; at the same time, through the scope which judges had to introduce limited reinterpretations and adjustments, it was susceptible of incremental change in response to changing social conditions. By contrast, statute was seen as a rather crude instrument, and one that had something inherently arbitrary and contingent about it. Instead of law emerging organically—sometimes edging in new directions, but always preserving coherence and continuity—it was *imposed* on the system in a way that was only too liable to create confusion and inconsistency.

Shortcomings of the common law

Bentham's assault on the common law was largely developed, in the first instance, by way of a critique of Blackstone's *Commentaries*. Indeed this critique, though he never completed it, was something he never abandoned: at the age of eighty he added some 300 sheets of manuscript to what he had written in the 1770s. There was something almost obsessive about his animosity towards Blackstone. Though he occasionally gave him credit for producing a serviceable map of the jungle of English law, he much more frequently denounced him; Blackstone had some claim to be regarded as an improver, of a cautious and modest kind, but Bentham described him in a memorandum of the 1780s as 'the dupe of every prejudice, and the abettor of every abuse' (B x 141). The personal misrepresentations, however, should not distract attention from the substance of Bentham's criticisms of the common law, which were expressed not only in the *Comment on the Commentaries* but in much subsequent work of a more general nature. He was not just attacking a particular interpretation of English law, but the foundations of a whole tradition and a whole orthodoxy.

One of his chief complaints about the common law was that its procedures, many of which had been evolved and adapted from practices of medieval origin, were very complex and technical. From the layman's point of view, they were largely unfathomable; and a particularly objectionable cause of their obscurity was an element of deliberate fabrication. Bentham took strong exception to the legal 'fictions' which had been resorted to as a means of adjusting the traditional system to new circumstances and needs. An example was the action of 'ejectment', which was commonly employed in order to get round a cumbrous procedure of feudal origin that was required for the proving of freehold titles. Because for leaseholders there was a simpler and more modern procedure for proving a title to landed property, a litigant wishing to claim a freehold title would assert that he had leased the title to a fictional person, and that this person had been wrongfully ejected from the property by another fictional person, who was the pretended lessee of the *real* person from whom the title was being claimed. Blackstone defended such fictions as useful instruments for overcoming inconveniences, and as evidence of the adaptability of the common law. But for Bentham, who was always deeply convinced of the importance, and utility, of truth, fiction was a kind of 'poison' which contaminated the system. By the use and acceptance of wilful falsehoods, the practitioners of the law were inured to mendacity; whatever fictions had done to ameliorate legal practices could have been much more beneficially achieved by straightforward enactments involving nothing in the way of pretence.

While this was an important source of disagreement between Bentham and Blackstone, a more fundamental one was their difference over the respective merits of common law and statute law. Bentham himself was critical of many aspects of statute law: he saw it as much too voluminous, as chaotically arranged, and as drafted in such a prolix and technical way that it was virtually incomprehensible to ordinary people. He also objected, as indeed Blackstone did, to much of the *content* of parliamentary legislation in the eighteenth century, and especially to the indiscriminate resort to the death penalty in penal statutes. But statute law did, in terms of form, correspond much more closely than common law to his idea of what law *ought* to be. He considered that laws should be—in fact he defined laws as being—expressions of the will of the sovereign or legislative power, supported and enforced by sanctions. The common law evidently lacked this positive and definite character. Indeed, he tended to treat it as one immense fiction, and a fiction that could not be broken down into determinate parts. There was no such thing as '*a* common law'; and he described the common law at large as a 'fictitious composition which has no person for its author, no known assemblage of words for its substance' (IPML 8).

Whereas the law ought to tell people in explicit and

unequivocal terms what it required of them, under the common law it was the judge who, in the light of the precedents, pronounced on the legality of an action after it had taken place. The common law was therefore, according to Bentham, 'judge-made'; and this meant that it not only contravened his own model, but also contravened the theory of the British Constitution, which assigned legislative power to Parliament. Furthermore, the common law was *ex post facto* law, or what he called in a famous analogy 'dog-law'. 'When your dog does anything you want to break him of, you wait till he does it, and then beat him for it' (B v 235). Only retrospectively and in relation to cases that had been decided could one have any certainty about what the law was.

Prospectively, its content in relation to any particular matter had to be conjecturally inferred from what seemed to be the relevant precedents; the common law consisted, not of explicit rules, but of 'general inferences deduced from particular decisions' (B v 5), and the content of its *implicit* rules was left for people to formulate for themselves at their own risk. In reality, of course, the vast majority of people had no means of doing this for themselves, because the precedents were buried in a vast mass of legal records, as well as in a legal jargon, which they had no means of penetrating. The citizen, unable to get at the law himself, 'is reduced to consultations—he assembles the lawyers—he collects as many opinions as his fortune will permit; and all this ruinous procedure often serves only to create new doubts' (B iii 206).

Doubts, according to Bentham, were inseparable from the common law because of its indeterminate nature, and because of the latitude which this inevitably gave to judges. On many occasions, he said, the judge was presented with a free choice. He could be rigorous in his interpretation of the law, or liberal: he could either ground his decision firmly on the precedents, thereby earning praise from his colleagues for his respect for established practice; or he could ignore the precedents and decide the case 'on the merits', thereby earning praise for his love of substantial justice. Bentham called this feature of the common law the 'double-fountain principle', the analogy being with a vessel used by conjurors out of which white wine or red wine could be made to flow at pleasure (B v 512). Adjudication under the common law, in other words, was inherently arbitrary and unpredictable.

The whole situation suited the legal profession extremely well. It suited the judges, who were to a large extent the effective law-makers, and it also suited all those whose legal training gave them a claim to be able to unravel the law's mysteries. A classic argument in defence of the common law was that it represented the long-standing, but always evolving, values and customs of the community, to which the judges merely gave declaratory expression. But Bentham saw it in a very different light: as reflecting and serving not primarily the interests of the public, but the interests of a professional élite. It was not surprising that lawyers admired and defended the system: they loved 'the source of their power, of their reputation, of their fortune'; they loved the common law 'for the same reason that the Egyptian priest loved hieroglyphics' (B iii 206).

The advantages of codification

For a time in the mid-1770s Bentham considered that it might be possible to give a tolerable degree of order and accessibility to the law of England by 'digesting' it. He thought that he might be able to produce a digest of the common law, which would than be converted into statute law through its being adopted by Parliament; and this exercise would be accompanied by a digest or consolidation of existing statute law. But within a few years he had become convinced that both branches of the existing law ought to be jettisoned completely and replaced by a code built on new foundations and in a new style. Thereafter, he took the view that English law books could only be useful to him as a means of checking the code's comprehensiveness: as a record, in his words, of 'the cases that are liable to arise and call for decision and therefore legislation'. Later he was to describe the value of existing *codes* of law in very similar terms (C vii 294; Dm. 33/I 159).

Although Bentham invented the term 'codification'—he

started using it in his letters in 1806 and in print about ten years later—the practice of code-making was much in vogue on the Continent during his lifetime and had, of course, a long previous history. It is clear from notes and summaries in his manuscripts that he had a considerable knowledge of the leading codes of his time, and he expressed qualified approval of some of them, including the Napoleonic codes in France; but none of them, he maintained, was really systematic or comprehensive.

One essential requirement of a Pannomion or comprehensive code, in his opinion, was that it should be actually enacted as law, as the will of the sovereign power. Its authenticity should be indisputably established through its emanating from the only valid source of law in the community. As for its content—here we are shifting from its formal qualities to its normative qualities, but Bentham himself regarded the two as closely interlinked—the most basic need was that all parts of it should be consistently aimed at promoting the public interest or happiness. An indispensable way of ensuring this, in his view, was to lay down that every provision should be accompanied by a short rationale in which its purpose and justification were explicitly stated. He appreciated that this requirement would add greatly to the difficulty of the enterprise: he wrote in 1822 that the production of 'an uniformly apt and all-comprehensive code of law, accompanied by a perpetually-interwoven *ration-ale*, drawn from the *greatest happiness* principle' could be safely described as not only the most important but also the hardest of all human tasks (B iv 545). Still, he considered that for the law to be what he called 'rationalized' was important in several respects. In regard to the legislator or legislative body, it would provide a continuous safeguard against any deviation from the path of utility in the process of law-making; in regard to the judge, it would help to ensure that there was no such deviation in the interpretation of the law; in regard to the citizen, it would help to fix in his mind the content and purposes of the laws he had to observe, and would gain his obedience 'not from a passive principle of blind fear alone, but with the concurrence of the will also' (B i 161).

As the last point implies, it was crucial that the law should be *known*, and widely and accurately known. Bentham underlined this in his letter to Madison in 1811 (in a sentence which is unhappily characteristic of his later style, and which may help to explain why the President took four and a half years to reply):

> On the fact of its being *present* to the mind of him on whose part, to the effect indicated, *action* or *forbearance* is, on each occasion, called for, *present*,— that is to say, in the degree of *correctness* and *completeness* necessary to the accomplishment of the legislator's purposes,—depends, on each occasion, whatsoever good effect the law can be, or can have been designed to be, productive of. (C viii 184)

Codification in general was vital for these purposes; and in particular, to make the law as accessible and what Bentham called 'cognoscible' as possible, effective promulgation and effective composition were both necessary.

So far as promulgation was concerned, it was important that the Pannomion should be arranged and made available in ways that were convenient for the citizens. It would be divided in the first instance into a number of codes. His enumeration of these was not always identical, but what he envisaged in 1817 was three main codes—constitutional, civil, and penal, with a corresponding code of procedure attached to each—and a number of subsidiary codes such as a commercial one, a maritime one, and a military one; later he favoured a somewhat simpler structure, with a single procedure code comprising the whole branch of 'adjective' (as distinct from 'substantive') law. In addition, for the purposes of distribution to private citizens, there would be a separate mode of division. A 'general' code would be compiled containing all those provisions that were of concern to citizens in general, and 'particular' codes would be prepared for groups of people in different occupations and walks of life, so that they could each have at hand in compact form the parts of the law that especially concerned them. All these selections would be published in cheap editions, and the general code would be made a subject of instruction in schools.

As for the composition of the law, Bentham wrote about this at some length in an essay published after his death under the title 'Nomography; or the Art of Inditing Laws' (B iii 231–83). In it he said that two of the chief imperfections to be guarded against were ambiguity and obscurity. He considered that special language and 'terms of art' could not be altogether dispensed with, and that some new terms would have to be introduced, for the existing vocabulary of English law compared with what it ought to be was like the vocabulary of astrology compared with that of astronomy. But all terms ought to be clearly defined, and always employed with the same meaning. He also said (though this was in an earlier work) that the sentences should be kept short, and that the style should be 'intelligible to the commonest understanding' (B iii 193, 217). Anyone who has tried to read the *Constitutional Code* will smile at these observations—though that work may deserve a marginally higher cognoscibility rating than the *Statutes at Large*.

The need for coherence and completeness

There were two further requisites of a general body of laws which were very important to Bentham, but which have been left until last because they need more explanation than others: that it should be systematically and coherently structured, and that it should be complete. These two requisites were in fact closely related. A systematic structure was not only essential for the general purpose of making the Pannomion intelligible as an ordered whole: it was also essential if the goal of completeness was to be achieved.

One important device which Bentham conceived for giving coherence and completeness to his *penal* code has already been mentioned, the exhaustive 'division of offences' in the *Introduction to the Principles*. But at the end of that work, when he addressed himself to the question of how his penal code would relate to the other parts of his Pannomion, he found himself faced with a number of questions. What was the relationship between penal and civil law? Were some laws penal

61

and some civil, or were all laws a mixture of the two? What, indeed, was *a law*? These questions had to be answered if the overall structure of the Pannomion was to be satisfactorily conceptualized. In this book there will not be space to follow Bentham far in his exploration of the 'metaphysical maze' into which these questions led him. But although he himself regarded his analyses in *Of Laws in General* as too rarefied to be of interest to the public, they did provide a theoretical underpinning for the ideas on codification which he expressed in print, and some of his findings are especially pertinent to the subject of this chapter.

One of the main purposes of his analysis was to show that all law—or all law that deserved the name—was fundamentally imperative. The unifying factor running through a properly constituted body of laws should be the *will* of the sovereign legislator. All parts of the Pannomion should represent that will; and at the heart of every individual law there should be a command or prohibition, almost invariably supported by a threat of punishment (though some laws might be supported by a promise of reward). He recognized that much of the law, especially in the so-called civil branch, was normally expressed in descriptive rather than imperative language; laws relating to property, for example, might seem merely to *describe* what constituted a valid title or how such a title could be legally transferred. But he maintained that 'law' of this kind was not logically complete in itself. Underlying all such matter there must be a mandate which prohibited any person, on pain of punishment, from occupying or interfering with a piece of property unless he had a title to it. Thus although for purposes of presentation it was convenient to divide penal and civil law, they were logically inseparable; and virtually every individual law could be regarded as having, and should be clearly shown to have, both a penal component and a civil or 'expository and qualificative' one, the latter defining the precise senses and conditions in which the act in question should be treated as an offence. ('Offences', for Bentham, included what are now termed civil wrongs, as well as crimes in the usual sense.)

By showing that civil law was not independent of penal

law, and by stressing the need for an imperative component in every individual law, Bentham was able to make it clear that legal matter of a civil or expository kind was related to the basic operations of command and prohibition. Also, he was enabled to maintain that his exhaustive division of offences, though originally intended as the basis for a *penal* code, could serve as the groundwork for a *general* body of substantive laws; and he concluded in the last chapter of *Of Laws in General* (234–7) that 'the catalogue of the laws is made out from the list of acts which are held up to view in the character of offences', and that 'by this parcelling out what relates to the several offences, the whole law is parcelled out'. He did not hold that the classification was complete in the sense that all the particular offences in respect of which particular laws might be necessary could be foreseen by the legislator. But he thought that all such offences would belong to *species* which did form part of the exhaustive classification, and that to identify them separately one would only need to add a stage to the process of bipartition. If stealing, for instance, was already an offence, but the legislator decided that stealing by night needed to be more heavily punished than stealing by day, the offence of stealing could be divided into two distinct offences, each of which would be made the subject of an individual law.

While the classification of offences was one important device for securing the completeness of the general code, there was another requirement that was vital for the same purpose. It was necessary that each individual law should be complete, in the sense of being framed in such a way as to minimize the need and scope for interpretation. Bentham held, of course, that a customary law was bound to be incomplete, not being expressible in a determinate fashion; but he also held that there were several ways in which a statute could be incomplete. For instance, it would be incomplete in point of *expression* if it lacked an imperative provision, while it would be incomplete in point of *design* if it was phrased too narrowly or too broadly to express the legislator's will satisfactorily. The example Bentham gave (OLG 161) was an old law of Bologna, 'Whoso draweth blood in the streets shall be severely punished.' This was on the one hand too narrowly phrased, in that it did not extend to wounding which happened to be unaccompanied by actual bloodshed; and it was on the other hand too broadly or indiscriminately phrased in that, taken literally, it would prohibit a surgeon from letting the blood of someone who was taken ill in the street. It was as a result of such deficiencies in the expressed will of the legislator that his 'real' will had to be divined and interpreted by the judge; in this way the power of the judiciary was enabled to grow up 'in the very cradle of legislative empire' alongside that of the sovereign; and customary law, 'striking its roots into the substance of the statute law, infected it with its own characteristic obscurity, uncertainty and confusion' (OLG 240).

In general, Bentham's craving for completeness arose from his fear that if any 'void spaces' were left in his Pannomion they would provide an opening for the introduction, in one form or another, of 'fictitious law' (B iv 537). He saw this happening in relation to the European codes of his own time: because of their incompleteness, they had to be supplemented by a mass of customary law and commentaries, and by the invocation of natural law and Roman law principles to determine doubtful points. If elements of this kind found an entry into his Pannomion, they would destroy all the benefits of definition and certainty which it was intended to bring. His desire to introduce certainty in place of uncertainty is worth reiterating. In his essay on nomography he said that the more uncertainty there was in the law, the greater would be the 'uncertainty of possession and expectation in regard to *property*', and the less security there would be 'for good in every shape, and against evil in every shape'. The most basic purpose of codification was to minimize uncertainty, and thereby to maximize security, which he described in this work as 'the great end of good government' (B iii 270–1).

The twin functions of law in general he saw as being to suppress wrongs and to define and secure rights; in 1830 he called his proposed penal code the 'wrong-repressing' part of his Pannomion and the civil code the 'right-conferring' part (CC i 4). In regard to their relative significance, he said (OLG 234) that 'in the order of intellection and enunciation'—in other words for clarifying the internal logic and coherence of the Pannomion—the penal branch might be regarded as having a certain priority; but in point of importance, he said, 'the civil branch (if it be possible to draw a line between matters so intimately and inseparably connected) might possibly be found to precede the penal'. The codification of penal law was clearly very important from the point of view of effective deterrence: it would tell people exactly what acts were unlawful and what punishments these would incur. But the codification of civil law—even though this branch of law relied on the penal branch for its 'obligative force'—was in a sense still more significant, as it was through this process that the whole framework of personal rights and civil relationships would be solidly and visibly laid down. By this means, each person could be given the kind of security that was based on a full knowledge of his rights and a confident belief in their being recognized and protected. The uncertainties—not to mention the expense—of the English amalgam of judge-made law and 'uncognoscible' statute law meant that, for most people, if not all, this kind of security was out of reach.

The role of the judiciary

An obvious question is raised by Bentham's attack on judge-made law and his advocacy of systematic codification. What role did he envisage for the judiciary under his Pannomion? This question leads us into some large areas of his jurisprudence that we have not yet touched on: his views on the linked topics of judicial procedure, the law of evidence, and adjudication. His writings on adjective law are even more extensive than his writings on penal and civil law. He left several thousand pages of manuscript on judicial procedure, and his *Rationale of Judicial Evidence* is much the longest of his works and (apart perhaps from the *Constitutional Code*) the most exhaustive in its coverage. Despite their importance for legal theory and practice, we shall only be able to indicate the main thrust of these writings, with particular reference to the role of the judge.

Adjective law in general was declared by Bentham to have two essential objects, between which there was inevitable conflict: one was to maximize 'the execution and effect given to the substantive branch of the law'; the other was to minimize the evils or hardships of various sorts involved in achieving the first object (B ii 6–8). He also said more specifically that the two ends of judicial procedure were, in the first place, 'right decision' (or avoidance of misdecision), and second, as a 'collateral' end, 'avoidance of vexation, expense and delay' (B ix 25). The main argument running through the writings on procedure and evidence was that the best way to achieve a satisfactory balance between the two objectives was to replace a 'technical' system of procedure with a 'natural' one.

The technical system was essentially judge-made: the rules and practices of the English courts had been shaped, to an even greater extent than other parts of the law, by judges and their coadjutors. And the character of the system was deeply affected by the fact that the judges and other officers of the courts had always been paid by fees rather than salaries. It was clearly in their interest—as it was in that of other professional lawyers—that the number of suits, sittings, transactions, documents, etc., which occasioned the payment of fees should be as numerous as possible. The complexities and artificial impediments of English procedure were thus mainly attributable to the 'fee-gathering system' and to the sinister interests of 'Judge & Co.'—the judges and their professional allies; and the obscurity in which the operations of justice were enveloped was largely a device for concealing the exploitation that went on, and for increasing the dependence of the public on lawyers.

One basic reform that Bentham advocated was the replacement of fees by salaries. He also wished to introduce a system of procedure that was as informal and uncomplicated, and hence as inexpensive, as possible. There were elements of the existing system that he wished to retain: he thought that the best way to establish the facts of a case was through oral testimony and cross-examination before a judge in a public court. But there was a mass of technical devices, requirements, and rules that he wanted to sweep away. He particularly objected to the 'exclusionary rules' which were part of the law of evidence and which prevented several categories of 'interested' people, including the parties to a civil suit and the accused in a criminal trial, from giving evidence and being questioned in court.

He considered that all such rules and privileges were obstacles to the discovery of the truth and should be abandoned, and that no evidence should be excluded unless the vexation, expense or delay involved in producing it was thought to outweigh its anticipated value. The proceedings of the courts should be modelled as closely as possible on the way in which a father would conduct an inquiry or settle a dispute in his own family circle, and the operative principle with respect to the hearing of evidence should be: 'Hear everybody who is likely to know anything about the matter: hear everybody, but most attentively of all, and first of all, those who are likely to know most about it—the parties' (B vii 599). It was up to the judge to prevent 'brow beating' by counsel, and also to take 'interest' into account when weighing the evidence given. On the general matter of the evaluation of evidence, Bentham was again of the opinion that rules were inappropriate; all that the legislator could usefully do was to provide the judge with 'instructions' indicating the various factors that he should bear in mind.

It will be apparent that in the task of establishing the true facts of a case the judge was to be given a large amount of latitude. Two further points bearing on his role should be mentioned. One is Bentham's belief in 'single-seated judicatories'—his belief that cases should be tried by one judge rather than several. The other is his lack of attachment to the traditional jury: he proposed that it should be replaced by a small 'quasi-jury' whose function would be to offer suggestions to the judge rather than to reach decisions. It is perhaps surprising, in view of his tendency to attribute so many of the evils of the existing system to judges, that he should have been willing to give them so much authority and discretion. Part of the explanation may lie in the fact that under the *Constitutional Code* professional lawyers—the 'whole train' of whose occupation engaged them in a 'perpetual endeavour to promote injustice'—would have been disqualified from becoming judges (B ix 392). (A fine stroke this from a Bencher of Lincoln's Inn!) Also, he believed that whereas the current system created a state of permanent opposition between the interests of the judiciary and those of the public, the situation would be entirely different once the institutional framework within which judges operated had been changed. Under the arrangements proposed in the constitutional and procedure codes, they would receive salaries from the state; publicity combined with 'single-seatedness' would make them plainly and individually responsible for their decisions; and they would be removable through a process initiated by complaints from the public.

It was also made clear in the *Constitutional Code* that in interpreting and applying the substantive law judges would be required to stick closely to the provisions of the Pannomion. 'Decision is right', Bentham said, 'in so far as . . . the will expressed by the law is conformed to'; and judges on appointment were required to make an 'inaugural declaration' which included the following pledge:

> I will on each occasion use my best endeavours to give execution and effect to every part of [the law], according to what shall appear to me to be the intent of the Legislature for the time being: not presuming on any occasion to substitute any particular will of my own, to the will of the Legislature, even in such cases, if any, where the provisions of the law may appear to me inexpedient: saving only the exercise of such discretionary suspensive power . . . with which the Legislature may have thought fit to intrust me. (B ix 25, 532)

It should be noted, however, that the last clause about 'suspensive power' did refer to an important role the judge could play in prompting revisions of the codified law.

Although the law would be explicitly and consistently designed to conform to the dictates of utility, Bentham recognized that cases would arise in which the strict application of the code as it stood would produce an outcome that conflicted with the greatest happiness principle. In such circumstances, the judge could not simply override the code, basing his decision on a direct appeal to the principle of utility. This would be tantamount to making or amending law on his own authority; and as well as contravening the authority of the legislature it would be opening the way to the development of a body of case law alongside the Pannomion. But what the judge could do was to postpone a final decision on the case, and to propose to the legislature, through the Justice Minister, an amendment or refinement of the law. If this was accepted (or not objected to by members of the legislature within a given period), it would be incorporated in the code, and the case would be decided accordingly. Similar provision was made for judges to propose amendments and extensions of the law, in order to remove ambiguities or obscurities, and in order to deal with matters not satisfactorily covered.

These articles in the *Constitutional Code* provide a partial answer to an objection that was often raised in Bentham's time to schemes of codification: that they would result in a petrifaction of the law and would preclude the kind of gradual change in response to changing circumstances that was characteristic of common or customary law. (Another part of the answer is to be found in the provision that members of the legislature should also be able to propose emendations.) One or two other objections which were raised specifically in relation to Bentham's scheme are worth considering by way of conclusion to this chapter.

Objections to Bentham's scheme

One objection related to his belief that his code would be suitable for a considerable range of countries; the criticism here was that his approach showed a naïve lack of concern about differences of historical background and social context. In fact, Bentham did give some attention to considerations of this kind in an essay written in the 1780s, 'On the Influence of Place and Time in Matters of Legislation'. He was not unaware of the historical or sociological dimension that was being given to the study of law by Montesquieu and by Scottish writers such as Lord Kames, and in this essay he specifically acknowledged the importance of Montesquieu's contribution. He also accepted that factors such as a people's customs, prejudices, and religion ought, up to a point, to be taken into account by the legislator. At the same time he stressed that his own approach was distinctive in being more exclusively 'censorial' or prescriptive than that of Montesquieu, who had sometimes 'confounded the question of fact with the question of fitness' (B i 180). Bentham himself was not particularly concerned about how geographical and social factors had, as a matter of historical fact, influenced and shaped the development of different social systems. What did concern him was how far these factors *ought* to affect legislation: how far the best legislation that could be devised would differ, from one country to another, because of them.

One of his conclusions was that some variations *would* be necessary in the legislative means of achieving the greatest happiness, mainly because of variations in what he called 'circumstances affecting sensibility'—in other words, because the actions that caused pleasure or pain in one country might not have the same effect, or at least might not have it in the same degree, in another country where the people had different customs and 'biases'. He suggested as an example, under the heading 'Offences against reputation', that to accuse someone of being a homosexual would not be regarded as a serious offence in a Muslim country, nor would it have been in ancient Greece; whereas in eighteenth-century England such a charge *would* cause serious damage to someone's reputation. He emphasized, however, that although customs and prejudices should be 'humoured', the legislator should not let himself be dominated by them; and if aggregate happiness would be increased by their removal he should do his best to sap their influence, by means of indirect legislation. The general outcome of his discussion was that in their implications for legislation the differences between peoples were much less important than the similarities; or, as he put it in his *Codification Proposal* of

1822, 'in comparison of the *universally-applying*, the extent of the *exclusively-applying circumstances* will be found very inconsiderable' (B iv 561). Human nature and human needs were to such an extent homogeneous that the framework of laws required for securing the greatest happiness of the greatest number would be found to be much the same for any territory, race or period; only in matters of detail would variations be necessary.

One should add that towards the end of his life Bentham's theory of legislation received a new though indirect challenge—and the defence of the English common law a new endorsement—from the emergence of a historical school of jurisprudence in Germany, headed by F. C. von Savigny. The message of this school was that the customary law of Germany was an endogenous product and reflection of the character and needs of German society, and that to replace it, as some jurists were recommending, by a system of codified law would be to sacrifice a vital part of the nation's heritage, ethos, and continuity. To understand and appreciate this legacy, and as Savigny put it to 'appropriate to ourselves the whole intellectual wealth of preceding generations', required a deep study of legal history. Bentham's reactions to the work of the historical school, which he knew only at second hand, were brief and dismissive (UC lxxxiii 156–60). He had recognized in earlier works that the past deserved some attention from the legislator because of 'the influence it preserves over the present and the future' (C/F 314), and because of the expectations that exist in people's minds as a result of long-standing practices. But he was inclined to take the line that history was of more value in showing what should be avoided than in showing what should be done; as he put it in *The Book of Fallacies*, 'It is from the folly, not from the wisdom of our ancestors, that we have so much to learn' (B ii 401).

One point that Savigny made in his tract *Of the Vocation of our Age for Legislation and Jurisprudence* was that the production of a complete code of laws was simply impracticable, because it would require the sort of organic unity that could only be generated by a single mind, and yet the task would be beyond the powers of any single person. Bentham was equally convinced that a satisfactory complete code would need to be 'the work of a single hand' (B iv 554); and some of his critics— and even some of his friends—felt that his projected Pannomion was hopelessly over-ambitious. Perhaps his own failure to complete it should be regarded as proving the wisdom of such doubts. On the other hand, the achievement of Edward Livingston in producing a complete set of civil, criminal, and procedural codes for the state of Louisiana showed how much could be done in this line by a single individual; and the extent of Bentham's own achievement in the 1820s suggests that if he had devoted himself as assiduously to codification in earlier decades, the completion of the Pannomion might not have been beyond his reach. There remains, of course, the question of how, if he *had* completed it, he could have got it adopted; but that is a question that belongs to the next chapter.

5 Constitutional theory

In most areas of Bentham's thought, there was a remarkable degree of consistency between the ideas which he formulated in the 1770s and 1780s and those which he expressed later in his career. In the sphere of politics or constitutional law, on the other hand, although there were some elements of continuity, these were outweighed by the marked change which occurred as a result of his conversion to democracy. This conversion was not a sudden one: it needs to be explained in terms of an accumulation of experiences and perceptions. But it did mean that in the last two decades of his life his thought had a different tenor from the one it had had in the age of the Enlightenment. Politically speaking, he not only changed with the times, but moved 'ahead' of them to a considerable extent.

We have seen that in the early part of his life Bentham did not devote as much attention to the constitutional branch of law as he did to the penal and civil branches; in his late, democratic phase he was apt to suggest that in his younger days he had been naïve in neglecting the political dimension and in imagining that those in power 'only wanted to know what was good in order to embrace it' (B x 66). It is true that in those early years he addressed himself mainly to sovereigns and legislators in the hope that one or some of them would be sufficiently impressed by his legislative schemes, and sufficiently motivated by benevolence or a love of reputation, to implement them on a large scale. But he was not as naïvely optimistic as he later made out. He wrote at some length in manuscripts of the 1770s about the obstacles that his projects would have to encounter; and he recognized that in England the vested interests of lawyers, who formed an influential minority in Parliament, would present a major problem. The fact that he was not entirely inattentive to political or constitutional issues is also apparent from the subject-matter of his first published work, *A Fragment on Government*.

Critique of contract theory

No doubt the primary purpose of this work was to weaken the forces of legal conservatism by confuting and discrediting Blackstone. But as well as demonstrating that Blackstone's reasoning was confused and specious, Bentham was setting up utility as the only proper and reliable source of legitimation in government, in opposition to the familiar doctrine of a notional contract, which Blackstone had restated. That doctrine had already come under fire from David Hume, who argued that the foundation of men's obligation to obey government lay not in any tacit promise or compact, but in the 'interests and necessities of human society' and in the fact that without such obedience society could not subsist. Bentham, too, wished to demystify the notions of political authority and obligation. He wanted to lay bare the essentials of a functioning political system, and to make it clear that it was only in terms of utility that the relationship between rulers and ruled could be meaningfully analysed.

He defined a political society as one in which some people, the 'subjects', were in the *habit* of paying obedience to a person or set of persons, the 'governor' or 'governors'. This habit of obedience could be weakened or eroded and could 'suffer interruptions', and the subjects could not be regarded as *obliged* to obey the sovereign power any longer than they saw it as being in their *interest* to do so: they could only be expected to obey 'for *so long as the probable mischiefs of obedience are less than the probable mischiefs of resistance*' (C/F 434, 444). If they were disposed to revolt, they would not be restrained by a 'fiction' or '*metaphysico-legal*' argument to the effect that they had somehow 'consented' and 'submitted' to the government they lived under (481). Something much more substantial would be needed to retain their allegiance, and perhaps the most basic message of the *Fragment* was that the best way to avoid an accumulation of discontent, leading conceivably to a withdrawal of obedience and a dissolution of political society, was to allow freedom of criticism and latitude for improvement—to allow, as Bentham himself put it, 'that liberty which is Reformation's harbinger' (406).

Most of the time, Bentham saw Blackstone's arguments—and especially his use of contract theory—as having a strong tendency to inculcate submission. Yet he considered that in one respect, in his invocation of natural law, Blackstone had veered to the opposite extreme. Blackstone said that no human laws should be 'suffered to contradict' the law of nature, and indeed that men were 'bound to transgress' any human law which did contradict it. According to Bentham, who regarded the law of nature as 'nothing but a phrase', 'the natural tendency of such doctrine is to impel a man . . . to rise up in arms against any law whatsoever that he happens not to like'. Blackstone, then, had signally failed to deal convincingly with one of the most difficult problems in the field of politics, the problem of 'adjusting the claims of those two jealous antagonists, Liberty and Government'. In Bentham's view it was only the principle of utility that could guide men safely through the straits between the two (C/F 480–3).

About the constitutional arrangements that would strike the balance most satisfactorily, Bentham was not very explicit at this period of his life. But from the *Fragment* and other writings of the 1770s and 1780s, some evidence of his views on the subject does emerge. For one thing, it is clear that he had little faith in the imposition of contrived limitations on the sovereign, or supreme legislative, power. It is true that he did not go as far as his follower John Austin did later in arguing that such limitations were impossible because nothing done by the sovereign could be said to be illegal. Bentham was willing to recognize that some situations might exist in which sovereignty was limited by 'express conventions', or by what he called in *Of Laws in General* (64–71) 'laws *in principem*': laws or covenants by which the sovereign power imposed limits on its own actions, and which were supported not by the political or legal sanction—for the sovereign power could not be expected to punish itself—but by the moral sanction, that is, the force of public opinion. (He gave as an example the Act of Union with Scotland, which had contained certain provisions declared to be binding on subsequent parliaments.) Nevertheless, he did not set much store by the imposition of a priori limitations on what the sovereign could validly do; and he said in the *Fragment* that the distinction between a free government and a despotic one did not lie in the amount of power lodged in the hands of the sovereign. The distinction turned, rather, on the manner in which, in a free state, power was '*distributed* among the several ranks of persons that are sharers in it'; on the source from which those who exercised power acquired their title to it; on the ease with which one set of governors could be replaced by another; on the extent to which the governors were accountable to the public; on the freedom of the press, and on freedom of association (C/F 485).

One should add, as it is a point of some importance for his political thought as a whole, that the phrase 'a free government' used by Bentham in the passage just cited was an uncharacteristic one, which he used only for the sake of its familiarity to his readers. In a manuscript of the 1770s he wrote: 'The expression a Free government, a Free constitution originates from the improper sense of the word liberty, where it is used for security against those in authority. The proper expression would be a popular government, a popular constitution' (UC lxix 153). He tended to equate liberty with the *absence* of government and law, and what was often referred to as liberty he preferred to treat as security: personal security against injury at the hands of other citizens, political security against maltreatment by those in authority. 'Liberty' for him was an emotive term, the use of which in politics distracted attention from the fact that it was essentially by restrictions on freedom that happiness was secured; in an early manuscript he compared the use of the word to drinking brandy: 'both cloud the understanding and inflame the passions' (UC c 170).

Critique of natural rights

It will be clear from what has been said above that Bentham was anxious to combat what he regarded as vacuous and delusive reasoning, whether it came from the right or the left.

His principal assault on fallacies of the left was made in the 1790s, in his extended critique of the French declarations of the rights of man. 'Anarchical Fallacies', like his attacks on Blackstone, contains some argumentation that might be regarded as merely captious, but it has none the less been described by Sir William Holdsworth, the historian of English law, as 'the most complete exposure of the logical absurdity of the doctrine of natural rights that has ever been written'. The famous 'Declaration of the Rights of Man and the Citizen', embodied in the French Constitution of 1791, stated that all men had indefeasible rights to 'liberty, property, security, and resistance to oppression'; and in the equivalent declaration in the Constitution of 1795 the 'rights of man in society' were listed as 'liberty, equality, security, and property'. These rights, said Bentham, were treated as anterior, and superior, to positive law: no law which infringed them was to be regarded as valid. Yet, expressed as they initially were in the form of *unbounded* rights, they were plainly irreconcilable with any workable system of law and government, and were also inconsistent with each other. To say, for example, that men had an unbounded right to liberty was to say that they could be subjected to no restraints whatever; to say that they had an unbounded right to property was to rule out the possibility of raising taxes; to say that they had unbounded rights both to property and to equality was (at least in any society where there was not a strict equality of goods) self-contradictory.

Later in the two declarations there were clear indications that the rights that had been affirmed so boldly and unconditionally were in fact intended to be limited. And how were they to be limited? By the law. This meant that the rights which were initially asserted *against* the legislative power were then left to be defined and limited *by* the legislative power. Bentham concluded that such declarations of rights were 'nugatory or mischievous', 'silly or pestilential'. They were mischievous or pestilential in so far as they set up natural rights *against* actual governments and positive laws. They were nugatory or pointless in that, while they *purported* to assert rights that legislators should never infringe, 'the extent of those rights in every direction [was] purposely left to depend upon the will and pleasure of those very legislators' (B ii 502). It was the mischievous aspect, of course, that Bentham was chiefly concerned about. He considered that the original declaration of rights had been framed to justify the revolution of 1789, and that by the way in which past insurrection was justified, future insurrection was invited. The whole tendency of the document, in which sweeping assertions about 'natural and imprescriptible' rights were given much more prominence than qualifying statements, was 'to excite and keep up a spirit of resistance to all laws—a spirit of insurrection against all governments' (B ii 501). For Bentham, the only rights that could be said to exist were *dependent* on law and government: a natural right was a contradiction in terms. As we have seen (p. 45), rights had no substance in his view unless they were protected by obligations; but in the declaration of 1791, he pointed out, obligations were hardly mentioned. He also wrote that the 'selfish passions', though in a sense necessary, were great potential enemies of public peace, and society was held together by keeping them under restraint: yet this document did its utmost to burst the cords that bound them.

Although Bentham thought that the vague and declamatory use of the term 'rights' in the French declarations was confusing and dangerous, and that the term should be reserved for *legal* rights, he did not deny that definitions of how rulers *ought not* to treat their subjects could sometimes be useful. But just as he preferred the word 'security' to the word 'liberty', so he thought that the term 'rights' in its political sense should be replaced by the term 'securities against misrule'. Indeed in 1822–3 he drafted a work under that very title. What he was considering in 'Securities against Misrule' was how far and in what ways, short of the introduction of representative institutions, the subjects of an *absolute* ruler could be provided with such securities; and he thought that it might be possible to persuade such a ruler that it would be in his own as well as his subjects' interests to allow publicity in official matters and freedom of discussion, and to grant a range of clearly defined securities against (for example) 'secret confinement' and 'official depredation'.

Such concessions would strengthen the ruler's hold on the respect and affection of his subjects, and, by promoting a 'general sense of security' in his dominions, would facilitate the growth of his subjects', and hence his own, prosperity (B viii 597). The concessions would of course impose some constraints on his own power. Since public attention would be focused on the points in question, he would be subjected to pressure from public opinion to honour the pledges given; and freedom of discussion would give feasibility to the ultimate sanction exercisable by the people over any ruler: the concerted withdrawal of the obedience on which his power depended. But the message here—not unlike that of the *Fragment on Government* forty-five years before—was that a dialectic between public criticism and governmental response would be a better guarantee of stability than any amount of repression. Bentham did recognize, however, in 'Securities against Misrule' that since the concessions made by the ruler would only be promises they would not be at all dependable. By the time he wrote this work, he had come to believe that the only *reliable* means of protecting the community against misgovernment was the establishment of representative democracy.

The need for representative institutions

The reasons for his adoption of political radicalism—first, ephemerally, in 1789–90, and again in 1809–10—were outlined in Chapter 1. His writings in these two periods are of great interest in relation to the evolution of his ideas, and his political pamphlets of the post-war years (1816–20) had some importance for the parliamentary reform movement. But it was in the last dozen years of his life that his theory of democracy was most fully developed and articulated, in the *Constitutional Code* and the writings related to it. In the early 1820s he presented his theory as based on three simple principles: the greatest happiness principle, the 'principle of self-preference' (see p. 25 above), and the 'junction-of-interests-prescribing principle'. 'The first declares what *ought to be*, the next, what *is*, the last the *means* of bringing what is into accordance with what ought to be.' It followed from the second principle that the *actual* end of any government would normally be the happiness of the governors; what was necessary to reconcile the second principle with the first was 'the bringing of the particular interest of rulers into accordance with the universal interest' (B ix 6).

The idea that people's *interest* needed to be artificially connected with their *duty* was one which had long been prominent in Bentham's thought. It was to be found in Helvétius and Beccaria, and lay at the root of his theory of punishments and rewards; and at an early stage of his career (as early as 1778, when he wrote his first pamphlet on prison management) he recognized its importance for ensuring that the responsibilities attached to official and managerial posts were properly discharged. Also, the idea that government should be considered as a trust was familiar to him from an equally early stage, and was indeed implicit in his principle of utility: upon that principle, he noted in a parenthesis in the *Introduction to the Principles* (263), sovereign power could 'never be other than fiduciary'. When he turned his attention to constitutional law and political machinery, these concepts were ready to hand, and in the writings of 1789–90 they led him in a seemingly inexorable fashion to the notion of *dependence*: the way to ensure that those who wielded political power executed their trust and performed their duty to the community was to institute a democratic electoral system which made them dependent on the community and liable to the punishment of dismissal.

The 'separation of powers', he wrote, though alleged to be a bulwark of English liberty, was in fact something of a myth, and even if it were a reality would not be an effective safeguard for the people's interests. He went on, in this manuscript of 1790:

The efficient cause of constitutional liberty or of good government which is but another name for the same thing is not the division of power among the different classes of men entrusted with it but the dependence immediate or mediate of all of them on the body of the people. (UC cxxvi 5)

Later, in 1809—in view of the influence exercised by the King and the peers over the House of Commons, and the lack of genuine popular representation in the latter—he described the famous mixed constitution of England as little better than 'a mixt despotism composed of monarchy and aristocracy' (UC cxxvi 408); and he said in 1817 that the King and the aristocracy between them formed a partnership, 'Corruptor-General & Co.', whose business consisted in 'draining the contents of all pockets into its own' (B iii 442). In the *Constitutional Code*—on the grounds that any portion of power given to a monarchy or aristocracy would inevitably be used to promote the interest of 'the one or the few' at the expense of that of the many—he argued for a system of government that was republican and unicameral as well as centred on a democratically elected legislature.

Sovereignty, in this code, was firmly located in the hands of the people, and was to be exercised by what Bentham called the 'constitutive' authority, that is, the electorate. The 'operative' authorities were divided into the legislative, the administrative, and the judiciary (the last two of which between them formed the executive). The elected legislature was to consist of a single chamber; for Bentham believed that a second chamber that was not elected democratically would have no justification for blocking the will of a chamber that *was* democratically elected, while a second chamber that was elected in the same way as the first would be superfluous. Also, there was no bill of rights in his constitution, and no system of judicial review; the legislature—though not sovereign—was declared to be 'omnicompetent'. However, having said that there were no limits to the powers of the legislature, he went on: 'In place of limits, it has checks. These checks are applied, by the securities, provided for good conduct on the part of the several members, individually operated upon' (CC i 42). The most important of these securities were those provided by the electoral system.

As the basis of this system, he adopted four measures that were commonly advocated at the time by radical parliamentary reformers: secret voting, manhood suffrage, equal electoral districts, and annual elections. He attached special importance—more than most radicals did—to secret voting, maintaining that without it the other measures of reform would be useless; for it was essential to prevent intimidation and corruption, and to ensure that the votes cast reflected the genuine will of the electors. Manhood suffrage he modified to the extent of making it dependent on the ability to read; he said that although this might seem at first sight to involve 'exclusion', it would not in fact do so because anyone who wanted the qualification could acquire it, with a little effort, in a short time (B iii 560). A property qualification, however, he did regard as involving exclusion, and he rejected any such provision on the grounds that 'the happiness of the most helpless and indigent [had] as much title to regard at the hands of the legislator, as that of the most powerful and opulent' (B ix 107). He would have liked to go *beyond* manhood suffrage in the sense of extending the vote to women: according to the greatest happiness principle, he said, women had at least as strong a claim to the protection afforded by the franchise as men did. But he believed that at that time a proposal to enfranchise women would arouse so much prejudice and ridicule that its inclusion would seriously damage the chances of his code being taken seriously. The last of the four main features of the electoral system, annual elections, was supplemented by a provision that at any time *between* elections members of the legislature could be 'dislocated' or dismissed by popular vote; and it was also laid down that those who had completed a one-year term as members would be barred from re-election for two or three years thereafter.

The members of the administrative authority and the judiciary were not to be directly elected by the people. These two departments were led respectively by a Prime Minister and a Justice Minister, each of them elected by and responsible to the legislature, and each at the head of a hierarchy of officials. Ministers were appointed and dismissible by the Prime

Minister, and judges by the Justice Minister. But these and a range of other office-holders, including the Prime Minister and Justice Minister themselves, could be individually dismissed if a petition for 'dislocation' was signed by a quarter of the electorate of any electoral district and was then approved by a majority of the electorate as a whole; so democratic controls extended to the executive branches of government as well as to the legislature. Moreover, the checks imposed by the political or legal sanction on both legislature and executive were intended to be powerfully supported by the force of the moral or popular sanction, as applied by what Bentham called the 'Public Opinion Tribunal'. This was public opinion envisaged as a kind of informal judicial body operating mainly through the press and public gatherings, and punishing transgressions by inflicting losses of popularity. To enable it to function effectively, regulations for ensuring publicity in legislative, administrative, and judicial proceedings were systematically laid down throughout the *Code*. Altogether, the wide range of more or less immediate checks exercisable by the public over the operative authorities seemed to Bentham to provide much better securities against misgovernment than any a priori limitations on the power of the legislature, or any provision that its enactments should be liable to invalidation by a body less representative of the people than it was itself.

It will be apparent that Bentham was determined to ensure that the ultimate power of the people was irresistible. And it *should* be irresistible, he thought, because only the people at large could have no 'sinister interest', no interest that conflicted with the public or 'universal' interest. Individual members of the public would of course be subject to the principle of self-preference and would have their own particular self-regarding interests. But in a democratic system of government the individual would have no opportunity of successfully promoting any interest of his own at the expense of the interests of others:

In so far as his aim is, to sacrifice all interests to his own,—
the interests of others, to that which is peculiar to himself,

no man finds any effective number of hands disposed to join with his: in so far as his aim is, to serve such of his interests alone, as are theirs as well as his, he finds all hands disposed to join with his. . . . The only interest of his, which an elector can expect to serve . . . is that which he has in common with all the rest. (B ix 63, 98)

One question which is ignored or skated over here—and it is a major gap in Bentham's democratic theory—is whether and in what way parties and pressure groups would be likely to operate under his proposed system. Another question is the one posed later by John Stuart Mill.

The tyranny of the majority

In his essay *On Liberty* Mill criticized Bentham (implicitly if not by name) for being so preoccupied with protecting the people against their rulers, and with counteracting 'sinister' or oligarchical interest in the operations of government, that he failed to appreciate that the people might need protection against themselves—or at least against a majority of themselves. What particularly worried Mill was the possibility that an ignorant majority would dominate an enlightened minority; and Bentham himself had expressed the same fear when he wrote in 1795 that democracy 'subjugates the well-informed to the ill-informed classes of mankind' (UC xliv 5). In 1810 he did produce a theoretical answer to this point. He said that if political power were placed in the hands of the few, the misgovernment that would result through the rulers' pursuit of their own interest was an evil which—human nature being what it was—could not be remedied. If, on the other hand, political power was placed in the last resort in the hands of the many, the 'intellectual imperfection' that might result was 'a weakness which not only admits of, but is every day enjoying the benefit of a remedy', through the spread of political knowledge and understanding (UC cxxvi 145–7). It is also relevant to note that in the *Constitutional Code* there was no question of the people at large being directly responsible for government or law-making, and regulations were laid down to ensure that both functionaries and legislators possessed 'appropriate intellectual aptitude'—before any person could qualify for public office or for a seat in the legislature, he would need to pass through a process of education and examination.

Another common fear about majority rule was that in a society which consisted of a minority of property owners and a majority of people without property, democracy would mean giving political power to the latter; the inevitable consequence would be the adoption of confiscatory or redistributive policies, which would undermine the security of property on which prosperity and economic growth depended. Bentham was conscious of this objection, which had been given some empirical support by the events of the 1790s in France. But in the early nineteenth century he developed two ways of countering it. One was to cite the example of the United States, and to point out that democratic government had been operating for decades in many of the American states without at all weakening the security of property. (America, indeed, supplied him with many arguments about the prosperity, efficiency, and economy associated with democratic institutions.) His other response, notably expressed in a work called 'Radicalism Not Dangerous' which he drafted in 1819–20, was that levelling schemes were so obviously impracticable, and so obviously damaging not just to the wealthy but to other classes of the population, that they would never muster enough support to be seriously attempted.

As for the *general* contention that democracy would entail a tyranny of the majority, we have seen that Bentham's shortening of the phrase 'the greatest happiness of the greatest number' to 'the greatest happiness' did reflect an awareness of the point. In an 'Article on Utilitarianism' which he wrote (but did not publish) in 1829, he said that if one divided a political community into a majority and a minority and specified that only the feelings of the majority should be taken into account, the result—which would be 'the more palpable the greater the ratio of the number of the minority to that of the majority'— would be to reduce rather than to increase the aggregate stock of happiness. For the minority might be made to suffer any amount of *unhappiness*, and Bentham believed that the quantity of unhappiness which any person could experience in a given period of time was greater than the quantity of happiness. As a practical example, he asked what the effect on overall happiness would be if all the Roman Catholics in Great Britain were made slaves of the Protestants, or if all the Protestants in Ireland were made slaves of the Roman Catholics. There could be no doubt, he maintained, about the answer (D 309–10). It does not appear, however, that when he was writing the *Constitutional Code* several years earlier he fully confronted the question of whether securities should be provided for the interests of minorities. He admitted that situations would be liable to occur in which, because the happiness of some conflicted with the happiness of others, it would not be possible for the happiness of *all* to be promoted; but he went on to say rather blandly that 'the phrase *universal interest* may be employed as corresponding indifferently to the interest of the greatest number, or to the interest of all' (B ix 6).

The means of achieving political reform

There remains the question of how the introduction of Bentham's *Code*, or the passage of any substantial measure of political reform, was in his view to be achieved. He continued, in the democratic phase of his career, to hope that in some country—perhaps Gran Colombia—a national leader might be found who would adopt his proposals in a wholesale fashion, even though their implementation would greatly curtail his own power. It was always within the bounds of possibility, Bentham thought, that an individual might be moved to act against his self-regarding interest. But it was much less likely, indeed almost inconceivable, that a body or class of men would voluntarily do so. He had no faith in the power of persuasion to produce such a result: relying on the force of argument to overcome the force of interest would be like using a peashooter against the walls of Mantua (B iii 507). At times he was so pessimistic about the possibility of inducing the English aristocracy to relinquish any of its power or privileges that he thought a revolution would be necessary. He was inclined to take this line at moments of indignation and discouragement when the government had displayed its ability to suppress radical agitation: after the suspension of Habeas Corpus in 1817, for example, and after the Peterloo massacre two years later. More usually, he held that it would be possible, sooner or later, to bring about radical change by means of intimidation. If a sufficiently powerful agitation were mobilized, the 'ruling few' might be made to realize that it was more in their interest to accept reform than to resist it. Bentham appreciated, however, that before a really strong and sustained agitation could be mounted, the 'subject many' would need to acquire a fuller understanding than they had yet formed of where their true interests lay.

His analysis of the means whereby this understanding was prevented from developing was one of the most original parts of his political theory, and one that in some respects foreshadowed the Marxist notion of cultural hegemony. He saw Britain, like most other countries, as governed by a partnership or confederation consisting of 'all the members of the government together with the opulent members of the different classes of the community in the character of persons unduly favoured by the laws and habits of government' (UC cxxvi 60). He sometimes referred to this élite as 'the ruling and otherwise influential few', and sometimes as the 'aristocracy', using that term in an extended sense to include not only the peerage and landowners but also various sub-groups, such as the 'lawyer aristocracy', the 'moneyed aristocracy', the 'spiritual aristocracy', and the 'literary aristocracy' (B iv 558 n). These confederated groups had a common interest in the protection of abuses and privileges; for people who profited from a particular species of abuse would naturally join in protecting other abuses, both 'on account of the mischief done in the way of precedent to their interest in any instance in which abuse in any shape receives correction, and in consideration of the assistance they may expect to secure in return, for the eventual protection of abuse in that special shape in which they possess their special interest' (UC cxxv 30).

As for the methods used to maintain the system as a whole, he did not underestimate the importance of military force. He said in 1817 that it was basically the standing army that prevented the people from trying to introduce a new system of government (B iii 443–4); and he always believed that a citizen militia was highly desirable as a barrier against political-cum-military oppression. He also attached considerable weight to the influence derived from various kinds of patronage and from the ownership of property. But the sort of influence he saw as particularly pervasive was that which the élite, through its manipulation of opinion-forming agencies such as the Church, educational institutions, and the press, was able to exert over the people's thoughts and sentiments. By such means, large sections of the population were imbued with loyalism or quietism, and with a generally deferential attitude to established authorities; and public opinion was distorted, and prevented from performing its natural role as a promoter and guardian of 'the greatest happiness'.

One of the main tasks that Bentham set himself in the last two decades of his life was to unmask the forms of exploitation that were being concealed by 'artifice' and 'delusion', and to spike the ideological guns of the élite by exposing the fallacious arguments and tricks of language that it commonly employed. One such trick criticized in the *Book of Fallacies* was the practice of instilling an automatic respect for certain categories of people in authority, irrespective of their behaviour, by saying that respect was owed to some impressive abstraction such as 'the Law' (instead of lawyers) or 'the Church' (instead of churchmen). Another was the tendency to appeal to 'the wisdom of old times' as if it was analogous to the wisdom of old people: in fact, said Bentham, 'old times' had less experience to draw on than later periods and ought in this sense to be called '*young* times' (B ii 398, 448).

It should be added that Bentham himself was liable to be accused—as he was by the young F. D. Maurice and by the logician (and later archbishop) Richard Whately—of using modes of argument which he branded as fallacious when used on the other side. In his sweeping and caustic condemnations of whole classes of people as irredeemably committed to the protection of abuses, he could be seen as using the kind of vituperative and 'passion-kindling' expressions which he had warned his readers to distrust. He did in fact anticipate this charge. In one of the last chapters of his *Book of Fallacies* (B ii 479–80) he suggested that the opponents of a pernicious policy might sometimes be driven to employ counter-fallacies against fallacies, and might defend this course on the grounds that it was the 'weakness of the public mind', rather than the weakness of their own cause, that compelled them to use such weapons as supplements to points of real substance. Whatever the merits of this argument (and it seems a dangerous one), there were certainly friends of his, such as the moderate reformer Sir Samuel Romilly, who felt that his own stridency in his later years detracted from the contribution he was making to the cause of reform.

6 Policy and welfare

One of the most controversial points in the interpretation of Bentham's thought has been the question of how far he was a believer in interventionism and even *dirigisme*, and how far he believed in *laissez-faire* and spontaneity. It is obvious that his theory of punishment was interventionist, in that the role of the legislator was to guide behaviour into socially acceptable channels by playing on the balance of human motives: by making it the *interest* of the individual to refrain from harming others. The role of the deontologist, in his theory of ethics, was less interventionist, for although it depended on the same analysis of motivation it did not extend beyond the provision of *advice*—advice about the ways in which the individual could maximize his own long-term happiness, including the ways in which he could do so by showing a regard for the happiness of others. The focus of this chapter will be on the areas of Bentham's thought in which the extent of intervention that was desirable for utilitarian purposes was most problematic—areas which would nowadays be assigned to the fields of social and economic policy, though he himself regarded them as aspects of legislative science.

Indirect legislation

One such area was what he called the 'indirect or preventative' branch of legislation, about which he wrote an unfinished essay in the 1780s. He considered here a range of measures which involved forms of government action apart from the enactment and direct enforcement of punitive laws. Some of the measures for the discouragement of crime would have meant a considerable amount of intervention or supervision in certain areas of life. They included, for instance, the regulation of trade in articles such as weapons and poisons, an extension of the practice of stamping goods for purposes of quality control and certification of ownership, and the use of tattoos or other markings as means of personal identification. He also wrote that one of the purposes of indirect legislation was 'to divert the current of the desires from objects in the pursuit of which men are more apt to be led into the track of delinquency, to other objects which are less liable to lead them into that track' (UC lxxxvii 62). Drunkenness and idleness, as major causes of crime, might be counteracted by measures to promote the consumption of non-alcoholic rather than alcoholic drinks; by the encouragement of 'innocent amusements' such as gardening, music, and games ('athletic or sedentary'); and by the prevention of unemployment, if necessary through the provision of public works. Also the moral sanction, source of the semi-social motive of the love of reputation, might be 'cultivated' through, for example, the circulation of literary material in which virtue was presented in attractive, and vice in unattractive, colours.

It has sometimes been suggested that in this essay Bentham revealed a sinister desire to promote the systematic conditioning of human behaviour. It should be made clear, however, that what he was doing in this work was not advocating a general programme for governments to adopt. He was putting together a miscellany of *possible* measures, many of them culled from the works of eighteenth-century writers on 'police' (a term that was then used with a wider meaning than it has today). He warned the reader that 'of all the expedients which may here present themselves to his view, there is not any one which I mean in this place to recommend as fit to be employ'd in any one nation in particular, much less in all nations indiscriminately'; the writer's object was not to recommend, but simply to 'bring to view' (UC lxxxvii 9).

Prisoners and paupers

Much clearer evidence for the existence of a *dirigiste* or manipulative tendency in Bentham's character is to be found in his writings of the following decade (the 1790s) on prisons and pauper establishments. His two schemes, the Panopticon penitentiary and the National Charity Company, have been briefly described above (pp. 7–9). The former was intended chiefly as an alternative to the system of transportation. When constructing his plan, he was aware that it was extremely difficult in penal matters to strike a balance between severity and mildness which would satisfy everyone: 'Some forget that a convict in prison is a sensitive being; others, that he is put there for punishment.' But he presented his plan as informed by three general principles. The 'rule of lenity' was that the 'ordinary condition' of the prisoners should not involve physical suffering or danger to health or life; the 'rule of severity' was that, with the proviso just stated, their condition 'ought not to be made more eligible than that of the poorest class of subjects in a state of innocence and liberty'; and the 'rule of economy' was that 'saving the regard due to life, health, bodily ease, proper instruction, and future provision, economy ought, in every point of management, to be the prevalent consideration' (B iv 121–3).

As for the more specific features of the system, it was to rest above all on the architectural device of central inspection. The jailer in his central lodge would be able to see into each of the prisoners' cells, but screens and lighting would be so arranged that he himself could not be seen by them; so although it was impossible in practice for each of them to be under inspection at all times, they would all have 'the impression of an invisible omnipresence' (B xi 96). The device, in Bentham's words, was 'a new mode of obtaining power of mind over mind, in a quantity hitherto without example' (B iv 39); it would also, of course, promote economy in that fewer staff would be required than in a conventional prison. Other features of the system were contract management, and the substitution of productive labour for the kind of 'hard' labour that was usually recommended for penitentiaries. The contractor, in return for an allowance per head that would be lower than the amount which the government would otherwise have to spend, would undertake to guard and maintain a certain number of prisoners, whose labour would then be at his disposal. The prisoners would work at ordinary trades, part of the proceeds forming the contractor's profits, and part being assigned on a piece-rate basis to the prisoners themselves, who could save it for the time of their release or spend it on supplementing the prison diet. Bentham hoped that as well as acquiring skills they would develop a habit of work, and even a taste for it.

To prevent the jailer from maltreating the prisoners, a variety of checks would operate; indeed, immediately after the sentence about 'power of mind over mind' quoted above, Bentham wrote that his plan would provide unparalleled security against the abuse of such power. The jailer would be required to publish reports and accounts, and to keep a record of punishments inflicted; as a protection for the prisoners' health, he would be liable to a financial penalty for every death in the penitentiary in excess of a certain 'normal' rate per annum; and the institution would be subject to more or less continuous inspection by the public. Facilities would be provided for enabling members of the public to observe everything that went on in the prison, and it would thus be exposed to supervision by 'the great *open committee* of the tribunal of the world' (B iv 46).

The plan for a National Charity Company to take over responsibility for the relief of the poor had a number of features in common with the Panopticon scheme. There was the same emphasis on contract management as the best means of reducing or avoiding public expense. Bentham maintained in an unpublished section of his poor law writings that in the public service there was a degree of patronage, inefficiency, and waste that would not be tolerated in a concern run on business lines; though he did also suggest that in due course the 'discipline of government' might have so far improved and 'outgrown its present habitual disease of relaxation' that state management might become preferable to a joint-stock company which depended on profits (UC cliv 547). Another similarity was that the Company, like the manager of the Panopticon, was to be given extensive powers over the people in its charge, though abuse of these powers was to be prevented by systematic record-keeping and unimpeded publicity. There was also the same emphasis on the extraction of labour from the inmates (under Panopticon-style supervision) to ensure the profitability of the concern; and the condition of those in the Company's workhouses was not to be made more 'eligible' than that of the independent poor. (Bentham did not, incidentally, go as far as the framers of the New Poor Law did subsequently in proposing that it should be *less* eligible.)

His general approach to the problem of poor relief differed from other solutions that were being put forward at the time. Some people were advocating minimum wage legislation, which he opposed on the grounds that it would increase unemployment; others advocated allowances to supplement inadequate wages, which he opposed as likely to undermine incentives and increase dependence on the rates. Others again were proposing that the Poor Law should be abolished altogether. Bentham believed that a system of relief was essential, as the greatest happiness principle required that everyone should be secured against starvation and the fear of it; and he argued that for the sake of efficiency and economy this system ought to be organized on a national scale. Moreover, the company he planned was not only to administer a privatized system of poor relief, but was also to make available, for the poorer classes at large, a number of low-cost ancillary services, such as savings banks and annuity schemes.

Despite the grandeur of the conception, however, Bentham's plan was open to a number of objections—as also was his Panopticon plan; and it is not surprising, either that both projects were abortive, or that the most indignant modern attacks on Bentham as a thinker have come from writers who have focused on these areas of his work. One major objection that has been made to both schemes is that although he declared himself to be aiming at a balance between the claims of humanity and those of economy, the latter were allowed to outweigh the former to a quite unacceptable degree. Prisoners in the Panopticon would have been required to work fourteen hours a day (which might have made it hard for them to acquire a taste for work), while a further hour spent operating a treadmill was to serve the joint purposes of providing exercise and generating power. As regards the amount of work required, and

the intensely regulated nature of the regime, workhouse inmates would not have been much better off than Bentham's
convicts.

He did maintain that the Company's paupers, and to a certain extent the prisoners in the Panopticon, would have had
some advantages which they would not have enjoyed outside
those institutions. In particular, they would have had security
in the senses of being free from want and free (because of the
checks on abuse of power) from oppression. He went so far as
to write, extending almost *ad absurdum* his interpretation of
liberty in terms of security: 'If security against anything that
savours of tyranny be liberty, liberty, in the instance of this
hitherto luckless class of human beings [paupers], can scarcely
ever have existed in anything near so perfect a shape'; the only
kind of liberty that would be ruled out was the kind that was
synonymous with '*lawless power*' (B viii 436 n). What Bentham is regarded as having overlooked in all this is the notion
that people—even in prisons, and *a fortiori* in poorhouses—
have some claim to be treated in a way that recognizes and
respects their status as human beings. It has been pointed out
as a fact of some relevance that one of the buildings for which
he thought the Panopticon design would be suitable was a
Ptenotrophium or gigantic chicken coop.

Some writers, furthermore, have argued that the defects that
vitiate these parts of his work are apparent also in his
philosophy in general, and indeed in the whole school or tradition of thought to which he belonged. Michel Foucault, as is
well known, saw the Panopticon—that 'cruel, ingenious
cage'—as a premonitory symbol of the repressive, disciplinary
society, the modern 'society of surveillance'. Another scholar
has described the Panopticon scheme as 'the existential realiza-
tion of Philosophical Radicalism', while another has suggested
that the National Charity Company might be viewed as 'a
microcosm of Benthamite society'. Some observations on interpretations of this kind will be offered at the end of this chapter.
But it is worth mentioning at this point a consideration
which may lead one to pause before assuming that the objections that can be levelled against his prison and Poor Law

writings are generally applicable to the rest of his thought. He may have had, as these writings suggest, an urge to control and regulate. But it is arguable that in most parts of his work such tendencies were restrained by his recognition of the principle that each man was normally the best ultimate judge of his own happiness and of how to promote it. In regard to prison and pauper management this control did not operate, since prisoners and paupers could be regarded as outside the circle of those independent beings to whom the principle applied. The chief problem he was tackling in relation to the management of such establishments was not how to maximize the inmates' opportunities for pursuing their own happiness with a minimum of mutual interference and injury; it was how to maximize the efficiency with which the institutions were run on behalf of the community at large.

Security

Before considering whether he was a *dirigiste* in regard to society as a whole, let us examine his views on some areas of policy which did concern the generality of citizens. In approaching the broad question of what governments could do to promote the welfare of those they governed, Bentham said that the overall aim of maximizing the happiness of the community could be usefully broken down into four subordinate aims: security, subsistence, abundance, and equality. Specifically, these were declared to be the proper ends of the civil or distributive branch of law, and also of political economy (though the latter was primarily concerned with the second and third of the aims listed). The different aims could, of course, come into conflict with one another; and priority, he said, should be given to security and subsistence.

In his 'Principles of the Civil Code' (drafted in the 1780s and published as part of the *Traités de législation*) he said of security:

This inestimable good is the distinctive mark of civilisation: it is entirely the work of the laws. Without law there is no

security; consequently no abundance, nor even certain subsistence. And the only equality which can exist in such a
condition, is the equality of misery. (B i 307)

He also wrote, in explaining why it was of crucial importance,
that it differed from the other objects of the law in that it
necessarily embraced the future as well as the present: 'security
implies extension in point of time, with respect to all the
benefits to which it is applied.' Previous jurists, he believed,
had paid far too little attention to the concept of *expectation*;
indeed the word itself was scarcely to be found in their
vocabulary. Yet the capacity to 'look forward' was a distinctive
endowment of man, and one that had a vital influence on his
condition; and the role of the law in securing expectations was
essential not only to peace of mind and to the pleasures of
anticipation, but to any 'general plan of conduct' or forward-
looking activity. It was the basic precondition, for example, for
economic enterprise and investment, and hence for 'abundance': 'any very considerable increase of wealth . . . is
altogether dependent on a general sense of security' (B viii
597). Also the concept of security extended laterally (so to
speak) to cover all the goods and interests protected by the law:
human life, person, reputation, property, and 'condition in
life'—by which he meant something like status (B iii 293).

Moreover, he envisaged the state as having a responsibility to
protect people as far as possible not only against intentional offences but also against accidental dangers and 'calamities'. One
of the government departments described in the *Constitutional
Code* was that of the 'Preventive Service Minister', who was
charged with implementing legislation for the avoidance or
mitigation of calamities such as landslides, floods, conflagra-
tions, and epidemics. Among other things, his ministry was to
concern itself with fire regulations and fire-fighting services,
surveys of bridges, dykes, and embankments, safety regulations in mines and factories, and measures for the repair or
demolition of unsafe buildings. He was to work closely with
the Health Minister in preserving public health, notably
through the provision of 'drainage in enclosed tunnels' for

sewage and by ensuring an adequate and uncontaminated water supply in urban areas (B ix 439, 444). Bentham also suggested that the state might provide hospitals for the sick poor and establishments for preventing disease through vaccination (S iii 361). It will be obvious that security required, in his opinion, a considerably wider range of governmental functions than was performed by the British state of his own time.

Subsistence

The second of his subordinate ends, 'subsistence', could be viewed as a branch of security; indeed he referred to it on occasion as 'security for subsistence' (B iii 295). But he regarded it as important enough to be separately identified, and he sometimes placed it at the head of the list on the grounds that without it nothing else was possible (S iii 309). As for the role of government in this regard, we have seen that in his opinion the relief of those without means of subsistence was a responsibility which the state could not ignore. He did hope in the 1790s that it could be devolved on to a joint stock company and that the system of poor rates could thereby be superseded. But in general he took the view that public provision for the indigent—those who lacked the necessaries of life—had to be made through a transfer of resources from those more comfortably off:

> The title of the indigent, as indigent, is stronger than the title of the proprietor of a superfluity, as proprietor; since the pain of death, which would finally fall upon the neglected indigent, will always be a greater evil than the pain of disappointed expectation, which falls upon the rich when a limited portion of his superfluity is taken from him. (B i 316)

In the latter part of his life, he was sufficiently influenced by Malthus to consider that if the poor were 'secured against death for want of the matter of subsistence' they would tend to add to their own numbers more rapidly than the rate at which the available matter of subsistence could be increased. Human benevolence could not be better employed, he said, than in seeking a 'reconciliation of a provision for the otherwise perishing indigent, with this continual tendency to an increase in the demand for such provision' (B iii 227–8). He believed that assisted emigration might alleviate the problem for the time being; but he did not suggest that a system of poor relief could be dispensed with. Indeed, in the *Contitutional Code*—where, incidentally, the idea of a privatized system is not mentioned—there is provision for a government department headed by an 'Indigence Relief Minister'. It is also worth noting that in order to safeguard subsistence Bentham was prepared during the French wars to approve two modes of interference with the market for provisions: as a temporary measure in times of famine, the imposition of a maximum price for grain; and as a more permanent measure the importation and storage, at public expense, of corn or rice which would only be released in periods of dearth. He wrote with reference to the latter proposal: 'Insurance against scarcity can not be left with safety to individual exertion. . . . Cost what it will, we can afford to pay for this as well as every other security that is to be had for money, and we ought to have it' (S iii 296). In the *Constitutional Code*, responsibility for maintaining 'precautionary supplies, in so far as freedom of trade is inadequate to the purpose', was assigned to the Preventive Service Minister.

Abundance

What about the extent of the government's responsibility for promoting 'abundance' or prosperity? This question opens up the whole field of economic policy, or what Bentham called the 'art'—differentiated from the more theoretical 'science'—of political economy. In some respects, and especially in his early writings on economic questions, he outdid Adam Smith in opposing interference with market forces. In criticizing Smith's defence of the usury laws, he said that there was no more reason to prevent a person from making the best terms he could in lending a sum of money than there was to prevent him from doing so in letting a house (B iii 4). In 'A Plan for an Universal and Perpetual Peace', written in the 1780s, he opposed all attempts to promote trade or particular branches of it through tariffs, bounties, preferences, or commercial treaties. Such measures did nothing to increase the country's overall wealth but merely influenced the directions in which capital flowed (B ii 550). The idea that the economic activity of a country was limited by the quantity of its existing capital, and that capital could not be artificially created by government but could only be increased by private saving, was also prominent in the unfinished 'Manual of Political Economy' (1793–5), where it appeared alongside the idea that individuals were much more likely than government agents to know in what branches of trade the available capital could be most profitably employed. Bentham examined a number of measures associated with the 'meddling or mercantile system' (S i 252 n) and showed that they were all either pointless or, more frequently, damaging; the only kind of intervention he treated with approval in this work, apart from the 'magazining' of corn, was the granting of patents to inventors.

Over the next few years he was much preoccupied with issues of currency and banking, and in this field he showed a greater willingness to look favourably on government action. He was concerned about the inflationary effects of the unrestricted issue of notes by country bankers, and he moved towards the idea that the issue of paper money should become, like the minting of coins, a government monopoly. Later this view was firmly stated in the *Constitutional Code*, where it was laid down that the 'money-making function' should be under the direction of the Finance Minister, and that he should periodically implement the wishes of the legislature as to whether 'the quantity of money of all sorts . . . should receive increase or not' (B ix 449). In his unpublished works 'The True Alarm' (1801) and the 'Institute of Political Economy' (1801–4), Bentham suggested that when unemployed labour was available an increase in the amount of money in circulation might increase national wealth by enabling productive enterprises to be expanded. Here—though he did add that when labour resources were fully employed an expansion of the currency would merely raise the level of prices—he was departing to some extent from Smithian orthodoxy.

He also distinguished himself from Adam Smith in his 'Defence of a Maximum' (1801), where he wrote that he himself had never had, and never would have, 'any horror, sentimental or anarchical, of the hand of government'. Smith, he believed, had sometimes opposed interference with market forces on the grounds that it was an invasion of 'natural liberty'; and in employing this argument—which could be used to invalidate any law whatever—he had fallen into a fallacy that was characteristic of the champions of the rights of man (S iii 257–8). Bentham himself did think that all forms of government intervention involved some degree of evil, because whatever the legislator did was bound to be 'felt in the shape of hardship and coercion somewhere' (S iii 311); but he said that whenever it could be shown that the advantages derivable from interference outweighed the costs, the measure should be regarded as good rather than bad.

None the less, in the 'Institute of Political Economy', which was Bentham's fullest attempt to write a handbook on economic policy, the general line taken—as in the earlier 'Manual'—was that there was little that governments could do in the way of actively and directly promoting 'abundance'. They should do their utmost, as we have seen, to promote it *indirectly*, through providing security: through ensuring that property and the rewards of labour were protected by the law. But otherwise the 'general rule' was that 'nothing ought to be done or attempted for the purpose of causing an augmentation to take place in the national mass of wealth . . . without some special reason'. The wealth of a community, the argument went on, consisted in the wealth of the persons who composed it; 'each individual bestowing more time and attention upon the means of preserving and increasing his portion of wealth than is or can be bestowed by government, is likely to take a more effectual course than what in his instance and on his behalf would be taken by government'; hence both individual and collective wealth could most effectively be increased by giving each person as much freedom as possible to pursue his own interest (S iii 333–4).

Bentham recognized that in a relatively backward country

there might be important things which individuals could not be counted upon to provide, and the government might therefore need to concern itself with, for example, the provision of docks, harbours, canals, and roads; but he seems to have thought that in advanced countries such things could usually be left to private enterprise. The *Constitutional Code*, which was intended to be suitable for a variety of states, included an 'Interior-Communication Minister' with 'inspective' and other functions, but the question of how far the transport system should be actually supplied and maintained by the public was left open. The same was true of the *Code*'s section on education, though Bentham did make it plain here that he wanted to avoid excessive control and dictation from the centre. The Education Minister was to be responsible for the educational establishments maintained by local authorities, corporate bodies, and individuals; but he was to take special care 'not to exercise any coercive or unnecessary interference, with the view of producing uniformity, contrary to the opinions and wishes of the parties immediately concerned' (B ix 442). One area where Bentham clearly did see the state as being able to provide a valuable service to the economy was in the supply of information. He thought that statistical and other data should be collected and made generally available; and he suggested in a footnote to the 'Institute of Political Economy' that establishments for the propagation of useful knowledge, like the Board of Agriculture and the Royal Institution, might be set up at public expense if there was little prospect of their being launched by the 'spontaneous exertions of individuals' (S iii 338 n).

Equality

The fourth and last of Bentham's subordinate ends was equality. As we have seen, he believed that given a certain quantity of any of the means of happiness (such as money), the more equally it was divided among a given quantity of people the greater their aggregate happiness would be. Other considerations apart, therefore, he was a believer in equality; but other considerations did in fact seem very important to him, and he saw equality as in some ways a dangerous rival to security, abundance, and even subsistence. He was consistently hostile to economic levelling, partly on the grounds that it was patently impracticable: 'an absolutely equal division of property could not subsist in a community of any extent for two days together' (UC cliii 153). If any attempt *were* made to establish equality on a permanent basis, the result would be the subversion not only of security and abundance, but also of subsistence, for all incentives to industry would be destroyed and no surplus would be built up to which recourse could be had in emergencies. He did occasionally recognize that a society might be organized on the basis of a community of goods. But he said that what happened in such societies was that in order to maintain production 'the gentle motive of reward' had to be replaced by 'the doleful motive of punishment', and two classes emerged, one of which used 'the cry for equality' as 'a pretext to cover the robbery which idleness perpetrates upon industry' (B i 312).

As for measures of redistribution which did not go to the lengths of *equalizing* property, we have seen that he favoured the raising of money from the propertied classes to provide for the necessities of the indigent. But although he countenanced this sacrifice of security to subsistence, he was unwilling to see security encroached upon for the sake of any move towards equality. He wrote in the 'Principles of the Civil Code': 'Equality ought not to be favoured, except in cases in which it does not injure security; where it does not disturb the expectations to which the laws have given birth; where it does not derange the actually established distribution' (B i 303). To justify this position, he used arguments of a psychological cast. He maintained that the prevention of the 'pain of disappointment' was particularly important for the happiness of those who had goods in their 'possession or expectancy' (B iii 226), and that those who had never experienced affluence would suffer much less from the lack of it than those who did possess it would suffer from its loss. He asserted, moreover, as a self-evident fact of human nature, that 'sum for sum, and man for man, the suffering of him who incurs a loss is always greater than the enjoyment of him who makes a gain' (S i 239). Although this principle did not invalidate the principle of diminishing marginal utility, it could be regarded as offsetting it to some extent in relation to possible measures of redistribution. Also, Bentham used the argument that was common in his time (it was used by Burke, for instance) that if redistributive policies were once embarked upon, even in an initially moderate form, there would be no means of stopping them from becoming progressively more extreme. He wrote in the 1780s:

> If, of two persons, the one is to take from the other a portion of the property he possesses to-day, because he is the poorer; for the same reason, a third should take a portion of such property from both to-morrow, as being poorer than either; and so on, till all security in the possession of property—all hope of retaining it, were altogether abolished. (B i 358)

The only deliberate ways of reducing inequality which he favoured were those by which security was either not damaged at all or only damaged very slightly, and what he particularly had in mind were measures concerning the disposal of property on the owner's death. He thought that some diffusion of property could be painlessly effected through the abolition of primogeniture and entails; and in *Supply without Burthen* (1795) he proposed that if someone died without close relations half his property should fall to the public, the other half alone being subject to bequest. In addition, he showed an interest in schemes to promote saving among the poorer classes; his annuity note proposal of 1801 envisaged a low-denomination, interest-bearing form of paper currency which would encourage saving among those classes not normally given to it. In general, however, he considered that governments could do little in a direct way to raise the living standards of the bulk of the labouring population. Even so, these classes seemed to him better off under a secure system of property than they would be otherwise. This was partly because their own means of livelihood were more secure. Also, in a society where (as a result of conditions of security) prosperity was growing, there was a *natural* tendency for inequality to diminish, because of the increasing opportunities for people to rise out of the labouring classes. He compared the social structure of European countries in his own time with that which had prevailed in the feudal period, when society was divided into a few great proprietors on the one hand and a multitude of serfs on the other.

A question that might well be asked is whether Bentham's conversion to political radicalism—to an equal distribution of electoral power—made any difference to his views on property. It is probably true to say that his more firmly 'conservative' pronouncements on the latter subject were made in the 1780s and 1790s. He said, for example, in the 'Principles of the Civil Code' that the legislator 'ought to maintain the distribution which is actually established' and that this function 'is with reason regarded as his first duty' (B i 311). Even if a different distribution could be imagined which would be more conducive to happiness, the risks to security involved in an attempt to shift from one distribution to another would outweigh any likely advantages. Later, there was some change in his tone. In an intended introduction to the *Constitutional Code*, he censured those who wrote 'as if man were made for property, not property for man', and who 'gravely asserted, that the maintenance of property was the only end of government' (B ix 77); and elsewhere he emphasized how desirable it was that the wages of labour should be maximized, because wage-earners constituted the vast majority of the population (B iii 230). None the less, equality remained at the bottom of his list of subordinate ends, below security, subsistence, and abundance (or wealth creation); and he did not follow Paine in explicitly associating political democracy with a programme of redistribution effected through graduated taxation and social services. He was more inclined to treat democracy as a means of *protecting* property—against depredations committed by the 'ruling few'—than as a means of redistributing it.

Bentham

Laissez-faire or interventionism?

His general position on matters of policy has been interpreted in a wide variety of ways. He has sometimes been presented as a proponent of *laissez-faire*, sometimes as a herald of the welfare state, sometimes as a harbinger of collectivism or 'statism'. He undoubtedly believed in *laissez-faire* to the extent that he considered private enterprise to be more effective than government action as the basic mechanism for promoting 'abundance'; and he also wished to get rid of certain inter- ferences with the market, such as the Corn Laws, which he regarded as unjustifiable products of 'sinister interest'. On the other hand, he was very aware of the need for certain kinds of intervention in order to minimize the costs of a capitalist system, and even in certain respects to supply the market's deficiencies. As a putative forerunner of the welfare state, his claims seem weaker than Paine's, but some of the principles he enunciated can be seen as pointing in that direction. In par- ticular, he recognized that in order to give people the degree of security he favoured, a considerable increase in state interven- tion and hence in administrative machinery was required. Here he was more realistic than Paine, who proposed a wider range of state-provided services than Bentham did, but did not face up to the bureaucratic implications. Bentham devoted a lot of attention, especially in the *Constitutional Code* and related writings, to questions of bureaucratic structure and technique, exploring ways of maximizing efficiency while minimizing expense, and emphasizing the need to establish clear chains of command and accountability.

He certainly envisaged a larger and more efficient state apparatus than existed in early nineteenth-century Britain; but are there solid reasons for considering that the kind of state and society he planned would have been oppressive and inimical to freedom? We have seen that in the constitution of his ideal republic there were numerous devices for ensuring that the 'ruling few' were responsible to the mass of the people, and it is also important to note that he was anxious to protect *individuals* against abuses of power on the part of bureaucrats;

the *Constitutional Code* included a substantial section called 'Oppression Obviated' which detailed the remedies available to citizens in cases of maltreatment or neglect by government officials. It is true that he was a believer in 'law and order', and that he also believed in surveillance (though carried out more by the public at large than by a Big Brother state on the lines of the Panopticon manager). But in his view there was nothing illiberal or unacceptable about legal or 'moral' pressures which led people to abstain from anti-social behaviour. He wrote in 'Anarchical Fallacies':

> The liberty which the law *ought* to allow of, and leave in existence—leave uncoerced, unremoved—is the liberty which concerns those acts only, by which, if exercised, no damage would be done to the community upon the whole; that is, either no damage at all, or none but what promises to be compensated by at least equal benefit. (B ii 505)

So far as acts of this description were concerned, the individual should be free to seek his own enjoyments in his own way. Bentham saw happiness as having two essential constituents: pleasures and security (IPML 347). The basic role of government was to provide the conditions of security in which people could pursue their own individual goals, their own pleasures, with the least possible unease and frustration. As he put it in the 'Principles of the Civil Code': 'The care of providing for his enjoyments ought to be left almost entirely to each individual; the principal function of government being to protect him from sufferings' (B i 301).

Expressed in this way, Bentham's aims seem unexceptionable. But a doubt that needs to be mentioned is how far his ideas on political and social organization (whatever his intentions were) would actually have avoided oppression and promoted individualism when put into practice. His whole strategy depended, in his democratic as well as his earlier phase, on the existence of a sovereign authority which was committed to the promotion of the greatest happiness, and which could therefore be safely entrusted with unlimited power. In his early years, he simply posited a sovereign

legislator on whose part this commitment was assumed. Later,
he transferred sovereignty to the people—in effect a majority of
the people—and made the same assumption about them. Indeed he argued in the latter case that he was not merely making
an assumption—for there were solid and obvious reasons for
believing that the people were disposed to pursue the greatest
happiness and could be counted upon to do so through the constitutive authority and the Public Opinion Tribunal. He did
concede that the public was not as enlightened on all points as
it might be, but he maintained that there was a general tendency
for its judgements to coincide more and more closely with the
dictates of utility, and that this tendency would be accelerated
as the propagators of delusion lost their influence. However,
some have questioned how far the public, or a majority of the
public, given the sort of political and social power that Bentham wished to confer on it, could have been trusted to respect
the demarcation he drew on utilitarian grounds between the
spheres of collective interference and individual autonomy.

7 Bentham and Benthamism

An attempt has been made above to set out Bentham's basic ideas on morals, law, politics, and social and economic policy, and to show the high degree of consistency which his approach—described by H. L. A. Hart as that of a 'cost-benefit expert on the grand scale'—gave to his treatment of these subjects. His method led him to some conclusions which, although unusual in his own time, seem much more acceptable or consensual in a modern context. It also led him to others which will seem as offensive to many people today as they would have done to his contemporaries. In the first part of this last chapter we shall draw attention to a few examples of both kinds, which have not been discussed earlier in the book. Thereafter, we shall consider some of the *general* reasons why large categories of people have tended to regard him with strong dislike; and finally we shall note the resilience and durability which, in spite of this hostility, his philosophy has shown.

One respect in which he anticipated later trends of thought—though he was not alone in doing so—was in his treatment of international law and issues of war and peace. His main writings on these subjects were not published until after his death and were not extensive; but his ideas, especially as restated in a well-known essay written by James Mill for the *Encyclopaedia Britannica*, had some influence on the nineteenth-century peace movement. He was not an outright pacifist, but he consistently treated war as 'mischief upon the largest scale' (B ii 544) and as almost invariably damaging to the peoples which engaged in it, though not perhaps to their ruling élites. He believed that democratic government, together with publicity rather than secrecy in the conduct of foreign policy, would do much to promote peace; that a spreading knowledge of political economy, and thus of the benefits of international trade, would have the same effect; and above all that the emancipation of colonies would remove one of the chief causes of international strife. He also had schemes for a code of international law, and for an international court which would pronounce on disputes between states and whose judgements would be backed by the moral sanction exerted by world opinion (BL 30151 15–18).

Another respect in which to modern eyes he was ahead of most of his contemporaries was in his concern for the political and legal position of women. As noted above (p. 82), he was cautious about including votes for women in his reform programme, because he was afraid that in the current climate of opinion such a proposal would have the effect of retarding the achievement of democracy for men. He also stopped short of recommending that women should be eligible for public office or for seats in the legislature. He made it clear, however, that in principle he favoured their enfranchisement. 'On the ground of the greatest happiness principle,' he wrote, 'the claim of this sex is, if not still better, at least altogether as good as that of the other.' The happiness and interests of women were just as important as those of men, and could be regarded as even more in need of protection; and a practical consequence that could be expected from the granting of votes to women, along with the secret ballot, would be an 'increased probability of the adoption of legislative arrangements, placing sexual intercourse [that is, relations between the sexes] upon a footing less disadvantageous than the present to the weaker sex' (B ix 108–9). Like John Stuart Mill later, he attributed the unequal treatment of women initially to men's superior strength, and more immediately to the fact that 'the strongest have made the laws' (B i 355). He also noted that conventions of decorum had 'castrated' the minds of women by associating femininity with ignorance; and that male domination was often explained in terms of women's intellectual inferiority, when that inferiority, in so far as it was real, was due to 'the abuse of that very power which it is brought to justify' (D 54; IPML 245 n).

A third example of his anticipation of twentieth-century thinking is the line taken in his unpublished writings on homosexuality. Blackstone in his *Commentaries* had placed sodomy under the heading of 'Offences against the safety of individuals'. Bentham, writing in the 1770s, observed: 'How a voluntary act of this sort by two individuals can be said to have any thing to do with the safety of them or any other individual whatever, is somewhat difficult to be conceived' (UC lxxiv 5). The law which made sodomy a capital offence, he suggested, was based partly on the authority of St Paul, and partly on an irrational antipathy such as lay behind the ostracism of albinos by certain Red Indian tribes. The only contemporary argument in favour of the law which seemed to him to deserve consideration on utilitarian grounds was the argument that if homosexuality were legalized there would be a decline in population. But he said in 1816 that it would be unlikely to have any such effect (as the experience of classical Greece indicated), and that if it did have this effect it would be a good thing rather than a bad, since over-population was the cause of much of the misery that existed in the civilized part of the globe. Into the scales against the existing law he put the real injuries to human happiness that resulted from it, including the actual punishments inflicted and the fear of such punishments, the repression of sexual instincts on the part of homosexuals, and the vulnerability of such people to blackmail: 'how easy it is to fabricate out of the dread of an accusation of this nature an instrument of extortion is but too obvious' (UC lxxiv 183).

Among other positions adopted by Bentham in applying his principle of utility, there are some which will seem, at least to many people, less congenial. Cases in point are his views on torture and infanticide. He was prepared to argue in his manuscripts that in certain circumstances torture might be justified, and that it could not therefore be absolutely proscribed. He did not endorse any of the ways in which torture was actually used in the Europe of his time, but he posited a set of general requirements which, if they were all met, might justify the use of torture to extract information that was vital to the public interest. It should only be employed, for example, if the case was such that no delay could be risked, if there was satisfactory evidence that it was in the prisoner's power to provide what was required from him, and if the benefit expected was sufficiently important to warrant the use of 'so extreme a

111

remedy' (UC xlvi 63–70).

As for infanticide, he was willing to condone, if not actually to defend it. What made *murder* in his view, a very serious offence was not the extinction of a human life, nor (principally) the pain suffered by the person who was killed, 'for that is commonly less than he would have suffered by a natural death': it was 'the terror which such an act strikes into other men' (UC lxxii 214). In the case of infants, the last consideration did not apply: the fact that some babies were smothered at birth would not create alarm and insecurity among other babies. To Bentham, the practice of condemning infanticide as a peculiarly 'unnatural' crime, and the laws which made it equivalent to murder, were grounded in antipathy rather than utility; in view of the stigma attached to illegitimate births, infanticide by unmarried mothers was quite understandable, and deserved far more sympathy than it received.

Some of the foregoing examples, together with earlier passages in this book, will have suggested one of the main directions from which hostility towards Bentham has often been voiced. To many religiously minded people, he has seemed a very sinister figure; and this is easily intelligible in view of the fact that, although he was cautious for most of his life about how he expressed himself publicly on the subject, his own dislike of religion was never hard to divine. His special antagonism towards the established Church derived initially from his being induced, against his inclination, to subscribe to the Thirty-Nine Articles while a student at Oxford. Many of the articles appeared on examination to be either meaningless or contrary to reason, and the requirement that students should subscribe to them before graduating seemed to him calculated to foster a 'prostration to authority' and an 'indifference to truth' (UC xcvi 287). Similar points about the Church's reliance on authority and obfuscation in propagating its doctrines, and about the damaging effects this had on sincerity and intellectual independence, were made by Bentham in his first published work on religion, *Church of Englandism* (1818).

The reasons for his animosity towards the established Church in the post-war period were partly political; but he was also very critical of religion in general, partly on moral and partly on epistemological grounds. He believed that the fear of punishment after death was largely ineffective as a means of deterring people from misconduct, but that religion none the less produced a great deal of repression and unhappiness, as well as intense dissension between the adherents of different faiths and sects. The philosophical reasons for his rejection of religion were never fully stated; but he maintained that all human knowledge was either positive or inferential, that inferential knowledge was inherently uncertain, and that the grounds for believing in the existence of God as a 'superhuman inferential entity' were so weak or non-existent that he ought rather to be regarded as a 'non-entity' (B viii 195–6).

Much of his writing on religion remained (and still remains) in manuscript, and his most radical attack on religion in general, the *Analysis of the Influence of Natural Religion on the Temporal Happiness of Mankind* (1822), appeared under a pseudonym. Still, it was clear enough from his main writings on ethics and legislation—especially from his consistent empiricism and his denial of any divinely implanted moral consciousness or divinely ordained moral norms—that the whole tenor of his philosophy was secular; and from an early date some of the most emphatic opposition to his thought was expressed by churchmen. José Vidal, a Dominican theologian at the University of Valencia, was arguing in response to Bentham in 1827 that since the Creator had endowed mankind with free will it was far from true that man had been placed under the 'governance' of pain and pleasure; and that if the truth of the latter principle were accepted, the notion of man's moral responsibility for his actions would be totally ruled out. In the 1830s and 1840s attacks on Benthamism were being made in England by leaders of the Tractarian Movement such as J. H. Newman. 'Surely', he wrote in his pamphlet *The Tamworth Reading Room* (1841), 'there is something unearthly and superhuman in spite of Bentham.'

Bentham's refusal to recognize a spiritual dimension to life was almost matched by his indifference to the aesthetic dimension. He did enjoy music, and the American minister Richard

Rush, visiting his house in 1818, noted that it contained three pianos. But Newman said in the pamphlet just quoted that Bentham 'had not a spark of poetry in him'; and although Bentham claimed to be able to tell the difference between poetry and prose—poetry, he said in a letter to Lord Holland, was where some of the lines did not go as far as the margin (C vii 570)—it is not surprising that he has often been condemned as an arch-philistine as well as an arch-secularist.

It is true that a remark of his which John Stuart Mill subsequently paraphrased and made famous—in Bentham's own words, that 'prejudice apart, the game of push-pin is of equal value with the arts and sciences of music and poetry'— was in fact expressed in a particular context. He was arguing against the granting of public subsidies to the arts: a practice which involved, as he put it elsewhere, 'laying burthens on the comparatively indigent many, for the amusement of the comparatively opulent few' (B ii 253; CC i 139). Nevertheless, the idea that if push-pin (a game not unlike shove-halfpenny) gave as much pleasure as poetry it should be valued just as highly was not out of line with his general opinion about matters of taste. He disliked the drawing of distinctions between good taste and bad taste, because he thought it could have the effect of reducing the pleasure that ordinary people derived from their favourite objects and amusements. 'There is no taste', he wrote, 'which deserves to be characterized as bad, unless it be a taste for some occupation which has a mischievous tendency' (B ii 254).

His views on education helped to create the impression that he had an uncivilized set of values. Though he himself had absorbed enough classical learning to trade quotations with the famous pedagogue Samuel Parr, he did not disguise his opinion that a knowledge of Latin and Greek was of little value to the great majority of people; and in his *Chrestomathia* (meaning 'useful learning') he drew up a secondary school curriculum for middle-class children in which the humanities were heavily outweighed by science and technology. To Hazlitt, this signified the 'grubbing up of elegant arts and polite literature' to make way for the 'systematic introduction of accomplished barbarism and mechanical quackery'; and many people since have regarded Bentham as the source of much that is soulless and materialistic in modern culture.

A third view of Bentham as a kind of *bête noire* is one that has been not uncommon on the political Left. It was most famously expressed by Marx, who had a gift for rudeness but excelled himself in his description of Bentham in *Das Kapital*: 'the insipid, pedantic, leather-tongued oracle of the commonplace bourgeois intelligence of the nineteenth century . . . a genius in the way of bourgeois stupidity.' One likely reason for Marx's severity was the fact (evident from his references) that he knew Bentham's work principally through Dumont's French editions, which presented the earlier and in many respects more conservative phase of his thought. It is also possible that Marx was influenced—as some later socialist interpreters have been—by the fact that after Bentham's death his ideas did come to form the basis, to a greater extent than he would probably have liked, of a distinctly middle-class ideology. In the 1830s 'philosophic' or Benthamite radicalism acquired a thrust that was much more anti-aristocratic than democratic or popular; it also came to be associated with the harsher aspects of political economy, and especially with the New Poor Law of 1834.

It is certainly true, however, that even in his radical phase Bentham's concern for the security of property meant that he remained by Marxist criteria essentially 'bourgeois'; and it is also true that his view of human nature was very different from Marx's. Although he did believe that with the progress of civilization there was a tendency for 'social' motives to be strengthened, he did not imagine that human psychology could ever be changed so radically that 'self-regarding' motives would cease to predominate. For Marx, the egoism and individualism which Bentham took for granted and built into his system were not permanent and universal features of human nature, but characteristics of man under capitalism. Marx had a vision of what human nature could, or rather would, be like—of how man as a 'species being' would achieve fulfilment in a communist society—which was much more optimistic than

Bentham's; and Bentham, for all his radicalism, was in the last resort conservative from a Marxist standpoint because he accepted man more or less as he was (or as he thought he was).

The impact of Benthamism

This book has been about Bentham rather than Benthamism. But we shall end it with a few remarks and suggestions about the impact of his ideas, and about some of the channels through which their subsequent development can be traced. On the influence of his ideas outside England, much research still needs to be undertaken, though some valuable work has been done in relation to certain parts of the world. In India, his legal theories helped to shape, among other reforms, the new penal code which T. B. Macaulay was largely responsible for producing when he was law member of the Governor-General's Council in the 1830s. In Latin America, as in Spain, Benthamism provided a secular and 'modernizing' ideology to which liberals such as Santander appealed for legitimation in their conflict with the forces of conservatism and Catholicism. It played a somewhat similar role in Italy—Cavour was fond of quoting Bentham—and in early nineteenth-century Russia, where Speranskii expressed admiration for his work on both legislation and economics (Dm. 7 76; 33/IV 217–18). In France and the United States, for a variety of reasons, his ideas had difficulty in achieving respectability, but in both countries his influence was far from negligible.

In the English context, his philosophy had to contend—to a greater extent than on the Continent, where it circulated in Dumont's relatively readable versions—with the obstacles which Bentham himself created by the style in which he wrote, especially in his later years. Paradoxically, it seems to have been partly through his efforts to be completely unambiguous that his style became so convoluted and opaque. A former secretary of his, Walter Coulson, wrote in the *Examiner* (19 October 1817): 'He seems every where to have laboured to express his opinions with a degree of accuracy, and a number of reserves, quite inconsistent with fluency. He has parenthesis within parenthesis, like a set of pill-boxes; and out of this habit have grown redundancies which become tiresome to the reader.' A Whig reviewer of the *Rationale of Judicial Evidence* described the style more bluntly as 'the Sanskrit of modern legislation' and regretted that it 'put such a fatal drag upon the progress of his philosophical opinions' (ER xlviii 458–61, 478). The drag was not actually fatal, however, because interpreters were not lacking to act as middlemen between Bentham and the public. In the early nineteenth century, as we have seen, James Mill played a somewhat similar role in England to that played by Dumont in relation to the wider world; and after Bentham's death the work of interpretation and diffusion was carried on by others, some of whom could be called 'Benthamites' while some made use of his ideas from more independent positions.

The extent and nature of his influence on legislation and government have been one of the most controversial issues in the historiography of nineteenth-century Britain. So far as the English legal system was concerned, it is obvious that his hopes for a total reconstruction were never fulfilled. But his contribution to the process of law reform was nevertheless substantial, and some of the outstanding agents in that process, including Sir Samuel Romilly, Lord Brougham, and Lord Denman, explicitly acknowledged their indebtedness to him. Among the changes which accorded with his ideas and which have been ascribed at least in part to his inspiration, one can cite the replacement of fees by salaries in courts of law, the simplification of the law of evidence, the establishment of county courts throughout the country to expedite the administration of justice, and the mitigation of the penal law.

As for policy and legislation in general, some rather far-fetched claims about his influence have sometimes been made, notably by A. V. Dicey, who curiously enough was a holder of the chair of law at Oxford which Blackstone had once held. In his *Lectures on the Relation between Law and Public Opinion in England during the Nineteenth Century* (1905), Dicey described the years 1825–70 as 'the period of Benthamism or individualism', and he attributed mainly to Bentham what he construed as the predominantly *laissez-faire* character of government policy in those decades. Since Dicey wrote, both the idea that Bentham was a believer in *laissez-faire*, and the idea that the mid-nineteenth century was a period of *laissez-faire*, have been challenged and substantially modified. Some historians, indeed, have seen interventionist elements both in Bentham's thought and in the actual trend of legislation after 1832, and have ascribed the latter at least in part to the impact of the former. Others have argued that the social and administrative reforms of the period were essentially shaped, not by the prescriptions of theorists such as Bentham, but by factors of a more impersonal and practical kind; according to this view the process of reform was a largely 'self-generating' one, resulting partly from a general growth in humanitarian feeling and partly from the pragmatic responses of men in official and ministerial positions to the concrete problems posed by industrial and demographic developments. However, while this is a useful correction to the Benthamites-under-every-bed interpretation, there can be little doubt that through avowed followers of his such as Edwin Chadwick and Thomas Southwood Smith, who were prominently involved in factory legislation, poor law policy, and public health, Bentham had more influence than any other social theorist on the growth of government responsibility in the middle decades of the century.

With regard to the latter part of the century, Dicey may have been nearer the mark than he was in his treatment of the earlier period. In a chapter called 'The Debt of Collectivism to Benthamism' he maintained that, through championing what amounted to untrammelled parliamentary sovereignty and majority rule and through savaging the concepts of a social contract and natural rights, Bentham had made an unintentional but significant contribution to the trend (which Dicey associated with the years since 1870) towards 'democratic despotism' and 'socialistic' policies. It is certainly true that Fabian socialists and 'New Liberals' of the 1890s and the early twentieth century—Graham Wallas, L. T. Hobhouse, Sidney

Webb—regarded Bentham as an important source of inspiration. It is also interesting that some recent critics of the social democratic welfare state—such as Anthony de Jasay in his book *The State* (1985)—have revived this aspect of Dicey's interpretation of Bentham's influence and have extended it deep into the twentieth century. Another writer, the Romanian exile and political scientist Ghita Ionescu, has described Bentham's modern significance in still more expansive terms. In his book *Politics and the Pursuit of Happiness* (1984), he represents the contemporary world as dominated by the confrontation between two ideological systems: the communist philosophy that originated with Marx, and the utilitarian liberalism that originated with Bentham. While disliking Marxism more than utilitarianism, he regards both as too materialistic; but he writes that 'no other ideology has ever enjoyed such a long continuity or such a universal impact as these two' (106).

In the overlapping fields of jurisprudence, moral philosophy, and economic theory, as well as in politics, recognizably Benthamic ideas have continued to feature prominently in debate since Bentham's time. In legal theory his most important follower was John Austin, who is commonly seen as the crucial figure in the development of the school of thought known as legal positivism—though H. L. A. Hart has suggested that if Bentham's *Of Laws in General* had been published earlier that book rather than Austin's less subtle and 'obviously derivative' work would have 'dominated English jurisprudence'. The thought of Hart himself, who is widely regarded as the outstanding legal philosopher in England since the Second World War, has to a large extent been developed on the basis of a critical reconsideration of issues raised by Austin and Bentham. He has departed from one major tenet of the positivist tradition, in regarding Bentham's imperative theory of law—and *a fortiori* the cruder version of that theory propounded by Austin—as inadequate for analysing the structure and operations of a modern legal system. On the other hand, he has upheld the positivist principle—which can be traced back to Bentham's distinction between the expository and the censorial aspects of jurisprudence—that law should be conceptually distinguished from morals and that analysis of law as it *is* should be kept separate from judgements about law as it *ought* to be. His writings on such themes have provoked widespread debate in the English-speaking world and elsewhere, and have been an important factor in helping to stimulate renewed study of Bentham. Recently, a 700-page volume of essays written mainly by Belgian scholars (*Actualité de la pensée juridique de Jeremy Bentham*, edited by Philippe Gérard and others, 1987) has examined from several points of view the 'astonishing topicality' of Bentham's ideas in relation to a range of jurisprudential issues, and has included some new discussion of the relationship between his thought and Hart's.

In moral philosophy, the utilitarianism of which Bentham can be seen as the classical exponent has shown considerable stamina. There were two notable restatements of the theory in the nineteenth century: John Stuart Mill's *Utilitarianism* (1863) and Henry Sidgwick's lengthier and more searching *The Methods of Ethics* (1874). Neither of them had quite the internal consistency and self-sufficiency of Bentham's theory, largely because they both set themselves a problem which his own philosophy was so framed as to avoid having to face. Both men differed from him in that they wished to establish that the principle of utility—or what Sidgwick called the principle of rational benevolence—should be regarded not just as the principle on which society ought to be governed or managed, but as the principle by which each individual should endeavour to regulate his own conduct; and neither produced a very satisfactory answer to the problem of how individuals who were disposed to pursue their *own* happiness could be expected to conform to a moral principle that was essentially altruistic. In the first half of the twentieth century, partly owing to some influential criticisms in G. E. Moore's *Principia Ethica* (1903), utilitarianism went through a period of eclipse, but in the second half of the century there has been a striking revival of interest. David Lyons's *The Forms and Limits of Utilitarianism* (1965) raised debate on the subject to a new level of refinement, and more recently R. M. Hare's *Moral Thinking* (1981) has been described as the most substantial formulation of utilitarianism since Sidgwick. Another scholar wrote in 1982 that utilitarianism 'may not be the most loved but it is certainly still the most discussed moral theory of our time'.

Bentham has also had an important influence on economics, though this did not derive principally from his own writings on economic subjects. Several of the outstanding 'classical' economists of the first half of the nineteenth century—Ricardo, James Mill, John Stuart Mill—were in certain senses followers of his. (Ricardo was largely converted to 'philosophic' radicalism by James Mill.) But Bentham's influence on these men's *economic* ideas was less marked than his influence on the neo-classical school of economics which emerged in the last third of the century. With writers such as W. S. Jevons and F. Y. Edgeworth, there was a shift from labour and cost-of-production theories of value to theories which highlighted utility, and particularly marginal utility. What R. D. C. Black has called 'Ricardo's predominantly physical approach to problems of production and distribution' was superseded by an approach which gave more prominence to psychological factors. Jevons and others drew explicitly on Bentham in developing doctrines which treated the maximization of utility—the achievement of the greatest possible satisfaction for consumers within the constraints imposed by available economic resources—as the basic concern of economics. Subsequently, the emphasis on utility, and the concern with attempts to measure it, have been dominant features of twentieth-century welfare economics. It is true that within this branch of economics Bentham's rather inchoate ideas about how utilities could be measured and compared have been much refined by some and substantially revised by others; and it is also true that the whole concept of measurable utility has come under fire from those who are sceptical about welfare economics in general. None the less, ideas whose provenance can be traced back to Bentham are as alive and controversial in economics today as in any other field of academic study.

Over the years, Benthamism has had to ride out a lot of stormy weather. It has had to survive, for example, the Romantic movement, the religious revival of the early nineteenth century, Dickens's *Hard Times*, the historical and evolutionist direction taken by much of jurisprudence and social science in the Victorian period, the philosophical idealism of the late nineteenth century, and the emphasis on the unconscious and the irrational in modern psychology. In the last decade or two, fresh assaults have come from sophisticated revivals of contractarian and natural rights thinking, and from the ideas of the 'radical right', which are seen as stemming originally from Adam Smith rather than Bentham. But although on several occasions it has been given up for lost, utilitarianism has so far managed to keep afloat; and it may well continue to do so for some time to come. It is still too early, however, to assess Bentham's prediction in a letter of 1824 that the Constitutional Code—the foundation of all his schemes—would be in force among all nations of the world by the year 2825 (B x 543).

Notes on sources

For the remarks by John Neal cited on pp. 16 and 18, see the introduction to *Principles of Legislation from the Manuscripts of Jeremy Bentham. Translated from the French of Étienne Dumont by John Neal* (2nd edn., Boston, 1830), pp. 95 and 22; and for Livingston's tribute, p. 17, see *The Complete Works of Edward Livingston on Criminal Jurisprudence* (2 vols., New York, 1873), i, p. 209 n. J. S. Mill's essays on Bentham, referred to on pp. 19 and 36–7, were published in 1833 and 1838, and the passages cited are in *The Collected Works of John Stuart Mill*, ed. J. M. Robson and others (Toronto, 1963–), x, pp. 77 and 15–16. The reference to A. J. Ayer on p. 27 is to his important paper 'The Principle of Utility' in his *Philosophical Essays* (London, 1954), pp. 250–70. For the quotations from Hazlitt on pp. 38 and 114, see *The Complete Works of William Hazlitt*, ed. P. P. Howe (21 vols., London, 1930–4), xi, p. 7, and xii, p. 249. Robin Evans's article on the Panopticon, cited on p. 38, is in *Controspazio*, no. 10 (1970), pp. 4–18. C. K. Ogden's observation on p. 45 is from his 'Forensic Orthology: Back to Bentham', *Psyche*, viii, no. 4 (1928), p. 5. The two unattributed remarks quoted at the end of Chapter 3 were made by Wesley C. Mitchell in *Political Science Quarterly*, xxxiii (1918), p. 182, and by Ian Budge in *American Political Science Review*, lxix (1975), p. 1434. For Sir William Holdsworth's comment on Bentham's 'Anarchical Fallacies', quoted on p. 77, see his *History of English Law* (16 vols., London, 1903–66), xiii, p. 56. The accusation, mentioned on p. 88, that Bentham committed what he had himself defined as fallacies was made by F. D. Maurice in his brilliant parody 'A Supplementary Sheet to Bentham's Book of Fallacies', *Metropolitan Quarterly Magazine*, i (1826), pp. 353–77, and by Richard Whately in his *Elements of Logic* (London, 1826), pp. 194–5 n. The quotation from Michel Foucault on p. 95 is from his *Discipline and Punish*, trans. Alan Sheridan (Harmondsworth, 1979), p. 205; and the unattributed quotations on the same page are from Gertrude Himmelfarb, 'The Haunted House of Jeremy Bentham', in her *Victorian Minds* (New York, 1968), p. 75, and Charles F. Bahmueller, *The National Charity Company: Jeremy Bentham's Silent Revolution* (Berkeley, 1981), p. 155. The observations of H. L. A. Hart on pp. 109 and 119 are taken from his *Essays on Bentham* (Oxford, 1982), pp. 24 and 108. For José Vidal's criticisms of Bentham on p. 113, see his *Orígen de los errores revolucionarios de Europa, y su remedio* (Valencia, 1827), pp. 287–8. Richard Rush's account of his visit to Queen's Square Place, mentioned on p. 114, is in his *A Residence at the Court of London* (London, 1833), pp. 286–90. The comment on Hare's book, p. 120, was made by R. B. Brandt in the *Times Literary Supplement*, 2 July 1982; and the quotation that immediately follows is from J. Griffin, 'Modern Utilitarianism', *Revue Internationale de Philosophie*, xxxvi (1982), p. 369. The quotation on p. 121 is from R. D. C. Black, 'Bentham and the Political Economists of the Nineteenth Century', *Bentham Newsletter*, no. 12 (1988), p. 28.

Further reading

The Works of Jeremy Bentham, edited by his literary executor John Bowring (11 vols., Edinburgh, 1843), is an inadequate edition in many ways, but is still at present the fullest collection of his writings available. A modern scholarly edition, *The Collected Works of Jeremy Bentham* (London/Oxford), has been appearing since 1968 under the general editorship of J. H. Burns, J. R. Dinwiddy, and F. Rosen successively, and under the supervision of the Bentham Committee of University College London. So far eight volumes of Bentham's correspondence have been published as part of this edition, and six volumes of his most important writings. Another serviceable collection is *Jeremy Bentham's Economic Writings*, ed. Werner Stark (3 vols., London, 1952–4). The writings on logic and language are brought together in *Bentham's Theory of Fictions*, ed. C. K. Ogden (London, 1932). Texts published for use by students include *Bentham's Political Thought*, ed. Bhikhu Parekh (London, 1973); the paperback edition of *An Introduction to the Principles of Morals and Legislation*, ed. J. H. Burns and H. L. A. Hart (London, 1982), which has an introduction written specially for this edition by Hart; and a paperback edition of *A Fragment on Government*, ed. Burns and Hart, with an introduction by Ross Harrison (Cambridge, 1988). For those who venture into the main collection of Bentham's manuscripts, the indispensable piece of equipment apart from a magnifying glass is A. Taylor Milne's *Catalogue of the Manuscripts of Jeremy Bentham in the Library of University College London* (2nd edn., London, 1962).

As yet there is no satisfactory biography of Bentham. The most impressive general study of his thought and its context is still Élie Halévy's *La Formation du radicalisme philosophique* (3 vols., Paris, 1901–4), translated by Mary Morris as *The Growth of Philosophic Radicalism* (London, 1928). Since the Second World War, however, and especially in the last decade or so, a succession of important monographs and many valuable shorter studies have appeared. The most comprehensive guide to the secondary literature in English is the bibliography compiled by Donald Jackson, which has been printed in successive numbers of the *Bentham Newsletter*, an annual publication initiated by Claire Gobbi under the auspices of the Bentham Committee in 1978.

A book which throws a great deal of light on Bentham's intellectual development, as well as on his specific contribution to the theory and practice of administration, is L. J. Hume's *Bentham and Bureaucracy* (Cambridge, 1981); the scope of the work is much wider than the title suggests. Publications which deal helpfully with several aspects of Bentham's work and its interpretation are Lea Campos Boralevi's *Bentham and the Oppressed* (Berlin, 1984), which covers *inter alia* his treatment of women and homosexuals, and David Lieberman's historiographical review 'From Bentham to Benthamism', *Historical Journal*, xxviii (1985), pp. 199–224. Mary Mack's *Jeremy Bentham: An Odyssey of Ideas 1748–1792* (London, 1962) is a study whose enthusiastic tone has led some scholars to overlook its frequent perceptiveness. Of short general introductions to Bentham's thought, one can recommend Shirley Robin Letwin's *The Pursuit of Certainty* (Cambridge, 1965), pp. 127–88.

On Bentham's moral philosophy, David Baumgardt's learned and capacious *Bentham and the Ethics of Today* (Princeton, 1952) is still useful; but a shorter and sharper study that can be strongly recommended, especially for its explanation of Bentham's theory of meaning, is Ross Harrison's *Bentham* (London, 1983). David Lyons, *In the Interest of the Governed: A Study in Bentham's Philosophy of Utility and Law* (Oxford, 1973), is stimulating but controversial. The interpretation offered in Chapter 2 of the present book is more fully developed in my paper 'Bentham on Private Ethics and the Principle of Utility', *Revue Internationale de Philosophie*, xxxvi (1982), pp. 287–300. James Steintrager's 'Morality and Belief: The Origins and Purpose of Bentham's Writings on Religion', *The Mill News Letter*, vi (1971), pp. 3–15, is the best introduction to that aspect of Bentham's thought.

The outstanding books on his legal theory are H. L. A. Hart, *Essays on Bentham: Jurisprudence and Political Theory* (Oxford, 1982), and Gerald J. Postema, *Bentham and the Common Law Tradition* (Oxford, 1986), which offers a challenging and closely argued reinterpretation of Bentham's 'utilitarian positivism' and his theory of adjudication. William Twining's *Theories of Evidence: Bentham and Wigmore* (London, 1985) provides a lucid exposition and discussion of another important area of his jurisprudence. A collection of papers which is still worth consulting on some points is *Jeremy Bentham and the Law*, ed. G. W. Keeton and G. Schwarzenberger (London, 1948). On the borderland between legal and political theory, see J. H. Burns, 'Bentham on Sovereignty: An Exploration', *Northern Ireland Legal Quarterly*, xxiv (1973), pp. 399–416, and the exchange between Twining and Melvin T. Delgarno on 'The Contemporary Significance of Bentham's *Anarchical Fallacies*', *Archiv für Rechts- und Sozialphilosophie*, lxi (1975), pp. 325–67.

A useful introduction to Bentham's political thought is James Steintrager, *Bentham* (London, 1977), and a work which focuses illuminatingly on a particular theme in his early writings is Douglas Long, *Bentham on Liberty* (Toronto, 1977). A valuable study of his mature political theory, centring on the *Constitutional Code*, is Frederick Rosen's *Jeremy Bentham and Representative Democracy* (Oxford, 1983). Essays on other aspects of his politics include Warren Roberts's two articles 'Bentham's Conception of Political Change: A Liberal Approach' and 'Behavioral Factors in Bentham's Conception of Political Change', *Political Studies*, ix (1961), pp. 254–66, and x (1962), pp. 163–79; J. H. Burns's papers 'Bentham and the French Revolution', *Transactions of the Royal Historical Society*, 5th series, xvi (1966), pp. 95–114, and 'Bentham's Critique of Political Fallacies', in *Jeremy Bentham: Ten Critical Essays*, ed. Bhikhu Parekh (London, 1974), pp. 154–67; J. R. Dinwiddy, 'Bentham's Transition to Political Radicalism, 1809–10', *Journal of the History of Ideas*, xxxvi (1975), pp. 683–700; Michael James, 'Public Interest and Majority Rule in Bentham's Democratic Theory', *Political Theory*, ix (1981), pp. 49–64;

and Pedro Schwartz, 'Jeremy Bentham's Democratic Despotism', in *Ideas in Economics*, ed. R. D. C. Black (London, 1986), pp. 74–103.

On social and economic policy, in addition to the works of Himmelfarb and Bahmueller cited above under 'Notes on sources', see the former's 'Bentham's Utopia', in her *Marriage and Morals among the Victorians* (London, 1986), pp. 111–43; Warren Roberts, 'Bentham's Poor Law Proposals', *Bentham Newsletter*, no. 3 (1979), pp. 28–45; T. W. Hutchinson, 'Bentham as an Economist', *Economic Journal*, lxvi (1956), pp. 288–306. On general methodology, see Douglas Long, 'Bentham as Revolutionary Social Scientist', *Man and Nature*, vi (1987), pp. 115–45.

Finally, studies of the reception and influence of Bentham's ideas include David Roberts, 'Jeremy Bentham and the Victorian Administrative State', *Victorian Studies*, ii (1959), pp. 193–210; S. E. Finer, 'The Transmission of Benthamite Ideas, 1820–1850', in *Studies in the Growth of Nineteenth-Century Government*, ed. G. Sutherland (London, 1972), pp. 11–32; William Thomas, *The Philosophic Radicals: Nine Studies in Theory and Practice, 1817–1841* (Oxford, 1979); Eric Stokes, *The English Utilitarians and India* (Oxford, 1959); Pedro Schwartz, 'La Influencia de Jeremías Bentham en España', *Información Comercial Española*, Sept. 1976, pp. 39–50; Theodora L. McKennan, 'Benthamism in Santander's Colombia', *Bentham Newsletter*, no. 5 (1981), pp. 29–43; my own survey (parts of which have been incorporated, with the kind permission of the journal's editor, in the present book) 'Bentham and the Early Nineteenth Century', *Bentham Newsletter*, no. 8 (1984), pp. 15–33; and Peter J. King, *Utilitarian Jurisprudence in America: The Influence of Bentham and Austin on American Legal Thought in the Nineteenth Century* (New York, 1986). A useful introduction to recent debates on utilitarianism among philosophers, economists and political theorists is Samuel Brittan, 'Two Cheers for Utilitarianism', *Oxford Economic Papers*, xxxv (1983), pp. 331–50.

Index

Index

OXFORD

MORE OXFORD PAPERBACKS

Details of a selection of other Oxford Paperbacks follow. A complete list of Oxford Paperbacks, including The World's Classics, Twentieth-Century Classics, OPUS, Past Masters, Oxford Authors, Oxford Shakespeare, and Oxford Paperback Reference, is available in the UK from the General Publicity Department, Oxford University Press (RS), Walton Street, Oxford, OX2 6DP.

In the USA, complete lists are available from the Paperbacks Marketing Manager, Oxford University Press, 200 Madison Avenue, New York, NY 10016.

Oxford Paperbacks are available from all good bookshops. In case of difficulty, customers in the UK can order direct from Oxford University Press Bookshop, 116 High Street, Oxford, Freepost, OX1 4BR, enclosing full payment. Please add 10 per cent of the published price for postage and packing.

BURKE

C. B. Macpherson

This new appreciation of Edmund Burke introduces the whole range of his thought, and offers a novel solution to the main problems it poses. Interpretations of Burke's ideas, which were never systematized in a single work, have varied between apparently incompatible extremes. C. B. Macpherson finds the key to an underlying consistency in Burke's political economy, which, he argues, is a constant factor in Burke's political reasoning.

'Professor Macpherson . . . teases out the strands in Burke's thought so carefully that one comes to understand, not only Burke himself, but his interpreters.' *Times Educational Supplement*

Past Masters

CARLYLE

A. L. Le Quesne

A. L. Le Quesne examines the views of this first and most influential of the Victorian 'prophets', explaining how his greatness lay in his ability to voice the needs of a remarkably moral generation.

'A first-rate introduction . . . it is not the least of the merits of this excellent short study that it shows some of the tensions yet to be found in reading Carlyle.' *Edinburgh University Journal*

Past Masters

MACHIAVELLI

Quentin Skinner

Niccolò Machiavelli taught that political leaders must be prepared to do evil that good may come, and his name has been a byword ever since for duplicity and immorality. Is his sinister reputation really deserved? In answering this question Quentin Skinner focuses on three major works, *The Prince*, the *Discourses*, and *The History of Florence*, and distils from them an introduction of exemplary clarity to Machiavelli's doctrines.

'without doubt the best short account of the author of *The Prince* that we are likely to see for some time: a model of clarity and good judgement' *Sunday Times*

'compulsive reading' *New Society*

Past Masters

HOBBES

Richard Tuck

Thomas Hobbes, the first great English political philosopher, has long had the reputation of being a pessimistic atheist who saw human nature as inevitably evil, and proposed a totalitarian state to subdue human failings. In this illuminating new study, Richard Tuck re-evaluates Hobbes's philosophy and dispels these myths, revealing him to have been passionately concerned with the refutation of scepticism in both science and ethics, and to have developed a theory of knowledge which rivalled that of Descartes in its importance.

Past Masters

ENGELS

Terrell Carver

In a sense, Engels invented Marxism. His chief intellectual legacy, the materialist interpretation of history, has had a revolutionary effect on the arts and social sciences, and his work as a whole did more than Marx's to make converts to the most influential political movement of modern times. In this book Terrell Carver traces Engels's career and looks at the effect of the materialist interpretation of history on Marxist theory and practice.

'Carver's refreshingly honest book . . . is packed with careful judgements about the different contributions of Engels to 19th-century Marxism.' *New Society*

Past Masters

COBBETT

Raymond Williams

Raymond Williams begins his book with a portrait of this extraordinary man, in one lifetime a soldier, a journalist, a farmer, and a political activist. But behind Cobbett's considerable personality lay important ideals and ideas. Professor Williams discusses these, and in particular Cobbett's views on poverty and property, on liberty, and on education, emphasizing the development of his outlook and identifying important shifts. He places Cobbett in context in the history of radical thought, and establishes the lasting importance of his tireless contributions to the debate about how society should be organized.

Past Masters